A BOOK OF OLD EDINBURGH

EDINBURGH CASTLE.

ST CUTHBERT'S, OR WEST KIRK, AND WEST PRINCES STREET 1820

A church has stood on this site since at least the eleventh century. This one was built at the end of the eighteenth century, and the spire is retained in the present church, designed in 1894.

A BOOK OF OLD

Edinburgh

COMPILED BY

EILEEN DUNLOP AND ANTONY KAMM

MACDONALD PUBLISHERS · EDINBURGH
LOANHEAD, MIDLOTHIAN, SCOTLAND

First published 1983 by
Macdonald Publishers, Edinburgh
Loanhead, Midlothian, Scotland

Selection, arrangement and notes
copyright © 1983 Eileen Dunlop and Antony Kamm

ISBN 0 86334 012 1

Design by James W Murray

Set in 11 point Plantin
Printed in Scotland by
Macdonald Printers (Edinburgh) Limited
Edgefield Road, Loanhead, Midlothian

Reproduction by
Morrison Scott (Studios) Limited
Crawley, Sussex

CONTENTS

5

Edinburgh from Arthur's Seat c. 1825

6

LIST OF ILLUSTRATIONS

(Plate numbers are in brackets)

✧

INTRODUCTION

EDINBURGH is a city of living history—for a start we have tried on the map on page 124 to demonstrate how many and which of the buildings illustrated in the book can still be seen, and within walking distance of one another. The city has been lucky too in its chroniclers. What first encouraged us to make yet another contribution to its literature was the realisation that many of the scenes and views engraved in the early part of the nineteenth century were those that the authors of the time would have known and had in mind when they were writing. The ensuing search, a combination of literary crossword puzzle and treasure hunt, had as its outcome this book.

We have tried to find appropriate illustrations for representative pieces by notable Edinburgh writers of the period, and some distinguished visitors, in prose or verse; and by Scott in both. One of the crowning moments in Scott's life is recalled as well, in the words of his author son-in-law. But Scott's 'own romantic town' was in the eighteenth century also one of the smelliest, as even Boswell had to admit. So Dr Johnson's classic remark as they walked up High Street is recorded, as are the appalling conditions in the wynds in the 1850s. At that time too, it is interesting to note, Edinburgh had, in Lord Cockburn and others, conservationists every bit as sensitive as, and perhaps more eloquent than today's.

Care in matching illustrations to texts also brought discoveries. The drawing of Charlotte Square not only includes the house in which Elizabeth Grant stayed in 1817 but could have been done at the same time. One of the views of George Street shows the row in which Shelley lodged after his elopement (today a wine-shop occupies his sitting-room!) And we feel we have captured, if at long range, a sight of Caddie Willie himself on the links to which he was devoted.

However the main purpose of the book is to entertain, and notes and extended captions are included where these might increase the reader's enjoyment of a passage or illustration. Students of history will find clues enough to follow up elsewhere if they wish to do so.

Our thanks are due to James Murray, our collaborator and designer who also adapted the map: to Miss Sheena McDougall and the other staff of the Edinburgh Room of Edinburgh City Libraries for their help and forbearance: and to William Heinemann Ltd for permission to quote the extract from Boswell's *London Journal* (edited by Frederick A Pottle).

EILEEN DUNLOP AND ANTONY KAMM

Dollar, January 1983

Edinburgh c. 1825 from site of present Royal Botanic Garden

ADDRESS TO EDINBURGH

ROBERT BURNS

EDINA! Scotia's darling seat!
  All hail thy palaces and tow'rs,
Where once, beneath a Monarch's feet,
  Sat Legislation's sov'reign pow'rs:
  From marking wildly-scatt'red flow'rs,
As on the banks of Ayr I stray'd,
  And singing, lone, the ling'ring hours,
I shelter in thy honor'd shade.

Here Wealth still swells the golden tide,
  As busy Trade his labours plies;
There Architecture's noble pride
  Bids elegance and splendour rise:
  Here Justice, from her native skies,
High wields her balance and her rod;
  There Learning, with his eagle eyes,
Seeks Science in her coy abode.

Thy sons, Edina, social, kind,
  With open arms the stranger hail;
Their views enlarg'd, their lib'ral mind,
  Above the narrow, rural vale;
  Attentive still to Sorrow's wail,
Or modest Merit's silent claim:
  And never may their sources fail!
And never Envy blot their name!

Thy daughters bright thy walks adorn,
  Gay as the gilded summer sky,
Sweet as the dewy, milk-white thorn,
  Dear as the raptur'd thrill of joy!
  Fair Burnet strikes th' adoring eye,
Heav'n's beauties on my fancy shine:
  I see the Sire of Love on high,
And own His work indeed divine!

There, watching high the least alarms,
  Thy rough, rude fortress gleams afar;
Like some bold vet'ran, grey in arms,
  And mark'd with many a seamy scar:
  The pond'rous wall and massy bar,
Grim-rising o'er the rugged rock,
  Have oft withstood assailing war,
And oft repell'd th' invader's shock.

With awe-struck thought and pitying tears,
  I view that noble, stately dome,
Where Scotia's kings of other years,
  Fam'd heroes! had their royal home:
  Alas, how chang'd the times to come!
Their royal name low in the dust!
  Their hapless race wild-wand'ring roam!
Tho' rigid Law cries out: 'Twas just!'

Wild beat my heart to trace your steps,
  Whose ancestors, in days of yore,
Thro' hostile ranks and ruin'd gaps
  Old Scotia's bloody lion bore:
  Ev'n I, who sing in rustic lore,
Haply my sires have left their shed,
  And fac'd grim Danger's loudest roar,
Bold-following where your fathers led!

Edina! Scotia's darling seat!
  All hail thy palaces and tow'rs;
Where once, beneath a Monarch's feet,
  Sat Legislation's sov'reign pow'rs:
  From marking wildly-scatt'red flow'rs,
As on the banks of Ayr I stray'd,
  And singing, lone, the ling'ring hours,
I shelter in thy honour'd shade.

EDINBURGH CASTLE FROM KING'S STABLES ROAD

PLATE 1

LAVENGRO

IT WAS NOT LONG before we found ourselves at Edinburgh or rather in the Castle, into which the regiment marched with drums beating, colours flying, and a long train of baggage-waggons behind. The Castle was, as I suppose it is now, a garrison for soldiers. Two other regiments were already there; the one an Irish, if I remember right, the other a small Highland corps.

It is hardly necessary to say much about this Castle, which everybody has seen; on which account, doubtless, nobody has ever yet thought fit to describe it—at least that I am aware. Be this as it may, I have no intention of describing it, and shall content myself with observing that we took up our abode in that immense building or caserne, of modern erection, which occupies the entire eastern side of the bold rock on which the Castle stands. A gallant caserne it was—the best and roomiest that I had hitherto seen—rather cold and windy, it is true, especially in the winter, but commanding a noble prospect of a range of distant hills, which I was told were 'the hieland hills,' and of a broad arm of the sea, which I heard somebody say was the Firth of Forth.

My brother, who, for some years past, had been receiving his education in a certain celebrated school in England, was now with us; and it came to pass, that one day my father, as he sat at table, looked steadfastly on my brother and myself, and then addressed my mother:—'During my journey down hither I have lost no opportunity of making inquiries about these people, the Scotch, amongst whom we now are, and since I have been here I have observed them attentively. From what I have heard and seen, I should say that upon the whole they are a very decent set of people; they seem acute and intelligent, and I am told that their system of education is so excellent, that every person is learned—more or less acquainted with Greek and Latin. There is one thing, however, connected with them, which is a great drawback—the horrid jargon which they speak. However learned they may be in Greek and Latin, their English is

OLD TOWN FROM THE CASTLE

PLATE 2

*Looking down Castlehill and beyond, to the crown of St Giles'
and the spire of Tron Church. This view was published in 1825,
less than ten years after Borrow was making this the start of his
daily route to school.*

execrable; and yet I'm told it is not so bad as it was. I was in company the other day with an Englishman who has resided here many years. We were talking about the country and the people. "I should like both very well," said I, "were it not for the language. I wish sincerely our Parliament, which is passing so many foolish acts every year, would pass one to force these Scotch to speak English." "I wish so, too," said he. "The language is a disgrace to the British Government; but, if you had heard it twenty years ago, captain!—if you had heard it as it was spoken when I first came to Edinburgh!"'

'Only custom,' said my mother. 'I dare say the language is now what it was then.'

'I don't know,' said my father; 'though I dare say you are right; it could never have been worse than it is at present. But now to the point. Were it not for the language, which, if the boys were to pick it up, might ruin their prospects in life,—were it not for that, I should very much like to send them to a school there is in this place, which everybody talks about—the High School, I think they call it. 'Tis said to be the best school in the whole island; but the idea of one's children speaking Scotch—broad Scotch! I must think the matter over.'

And he did think the matter over; and the result of his deliberation was a determination to send us to the school. Let me call thee up before my mind's eye, High School, to which, every morning, the two English brothers took their way from the proud old Castle through the lofty streets of the Old Town. High School!—called so, I scarcely know why; neither lofty in thyself nor by position, being situated in a flat bottom; oblong structure of tawny stone, with many windows fenced with iron netting—with thy long hall below, and thy five chambers above, for the reception of the five classes, into which the eight hundred urchins, who styled thee instructress, were divided. Thy learned rector and his four subordinate dominies; thy strange old porter of the tall form and grizzled hair, hight Boee, and doubtless of Norse ancestry, as his name declares; perhaps of the blood of Bui hin Digri, the hero of northern song—the Jomsborg Viking who clove Thorsteinn Midlaagr asunder in the dread sea battle of Horunga Vog, and who, when the fight was lost and his own two hands smitten off, seized two chests of gold with his bloody stumps, and, springing with them into the sea, cried to the scanty relics of his crew, 'Overboard now, all Bui's lads!' Yes, I remember all about thee, and how at eight of every morn we were all gathered together with one accord in the long hall, from which, after the litanies had been read (for so I call them, being an Episcopalian), the five classes from the five sets of benches trotted off in long files, one boy after the other, up the five spiral staircases of stone, each class

HIGH SCHOOL WYND

PLATE 3

Looking back from the direction of the school gates across
Cowgate to the bottom of Blackfriars' Wynd.

to its destination; and well do I remember how we of the third sat hushed and still, watched by the eye of the dux, until the door opened, and in walked that model of a good Scotchman, the shrewd, intelligent, but warm-hearted and kind dominie, the respectable Carson.

And in this school I began to construe the Latin language, which I had never done before, notwithstanding my long and diligent study of Lilly, which illustrious grammar was not used at Edinburgh, nor indeed known. Greek was only taught in the fifth or highest class, in which my brother was; as for myself, I never got beyond the third during the two years that I remained at this seminary. I certainly acquired here a considerable insight in the Latin tongue; and, to the scandal of my father and horror of my mother, a thorough proficiency of the Scotch, which, in less than two months, usurped the place of the English, and so obstinately maintained its ground, that I still can occasionally detect its lingering remains. I did not spend my time unpleasantly at this school, though, first of all, I had to pass through an ordeal.

'Scotland is a better country than England,' said an ugly, blear-eyed lad, about a head and shoulders taller than myself, the leader of a gang of varlets who surrounded me in the playground, on the first day, as soon as the morning lesson was over. 'Scotland is a far better country than England, in every respect.'

'Is it?' said I. 'Then you ought to be very thankful for not having been born in England.'

'That's just what I am, ye loon; and every morning when I say my prayers, I thank God for not being an Englishman. The Scotch are a much better and braver people than the English.'

'It may be so,' said I, 'for what I know—indeed, till I came here, I never heard a word either about the Scotch or their country.'

'Are ye making fun of us, ye English puppy?' said the blear-eyed lad; 'take that!' and I was presently beaten black and blue. And thus did I first become aware of the difference of races and their antipathy to each other.

'Bow to the storm, and it shall pass over you.' I held my peace, and silently submitted to the superiority of the Scotch—*in numbers*. This was enough; from an object of persecution I soon became one of patronage, especially amongst the champions of the class. 'The English,' said the blear-eyed lad, 'though a wee bit behind the Scotch in strength and fortitude, are nae to be sneezed at, being far ahead of the Irish, to say nothing of the French, a pack of cowardly scoundrels. And with regard to the English country, it is na Scotland, it is true, but it has its gude properties; and, though there is ne'er a haggis in a' the land, there's an unco deal o' gowd and siller. I respect England, for I have an auntie married there.'

HIGH SCHOOL

PLATE 4

*This building (now reconstructed) housed the school from 1778 to
1829, when the new school on Calton Hill was finished. Lord
Cockburn, Henry Mackenzie and Sir Walter Scott were former
pupils, and were among those who energetically advocated the
founding in 1824 of the rival Edinburgh Academy.*

BLACKFRIARS' WYND ANALYZED

GEORGE BELL

AT THE END of the low and narrow passage out of which these chambers open, we found another minute room, of irregular shape, inhabited by three women and a dog, which savagely attacked us. One of these women is twenty-three years of age, and has been married for six years. Her husband has deserted her several times, and she has not seen him for two years. He is now in Glasgow working; but he never sends her any money. The mother of this young woman kept a dram-shop, and she acted the part of a servant. Three months after the death of her mother, her father married again, and the stepmother and stepdaughter began to quarrel. The stepdaughter says that she has beat her stepmother several times, broken the windows, and smashed the crockery; and she justifies these proceedings on the ground, that the stepmother now possesses what, she thinks, ought to belong to her—namely, her late mother's property. In the mean time, she has been turned out of doors; but her child, which is eighteen months old, is taken charge of by her father. She can read, write, and sew, and declares that she is a very sober and well-disposed person. She looks, however, what she is—a vindictive and depraved young woman. She knows what is right, and professes to have a desire to do well; but it is all too evident that she is shamefully wicked—that she is a notorious drunkard—and that she has been several times in custody. An old woman over whose head many years of cinder-gathering have passed—who is now literally clothed in dust and ashes—who 'taks a dram hersel', but no' to do her ony ill,' held up her mole-like hands, and said with an expression of, we know not what—for it was hid under accumulated deposits of dirt and smoke—that this young person 'is a drucken blackguard woman, and that she can have no *correspondence* with her.' The sentiments of this old woman, it may be supposed, are not very refined, and the subject may well be regarded as a very bad one, who is contemned and spurned by her. This ancient cinder-woman deserves to be noticed somewhat approvingly. She is the widow of a soldier, and has an only daughter, whose early misconduct was the cause of the old woman's descent to the lowest level. The mother would not desert the daughter, and therefore her customers deserted her. From being a respectable washerwoman, she has gradually sunk to the position which she now occupies, and, instead of being supported by her daughter, she supports her daughter's natural child, a girl of fifteen years of age, whose origin and present position are barriers in the way of her getting employment. In addition to this, she has lately taken one of her grandsons, born in wedlock, under her protection. The tatters and starved look of the little lad proved that his grandmother could do but little for him; and learning that he had never been at school, and seeing that there was no prospect of his being sent, we transplanted him from the wynd into the Original Ragged School, where we hope to see him grow up a good and useful member of society. The garret which this old woman occupies is very small, and very wretched; yet it shelters two adults and three children.

BLACKFRIARS' WYND 1837

PLATE 5

As it was thirteen years before Bell's report was published.

CATRIONA

ROBERT LOUIS STEVENSON

BEING STRANGE to what I saw, I stepped a little farther in. The narrow paved way descended swiftly. Prodigious tall houses sprang upon each side and bulged out, one storey beyond another, as they rose. At the top only a ribbon of sky showed in. By what I could spy in the windows, and by the respectable persons that passed out and in, I saw the houses to be very well occupied; and the whole appearance of the place interested me like a tale.

I was still gazing, when there came a sudden brisk tramp of feet in time and clash of steel behind me. Turning quickly, I was aware of a party of armed soldiers, and, in their midst, a tall man in a great-coat. He walked with a stoop that was like a piece of courtesy, genteel and insinuating: he waved his hand plausibly as he went, and his face was sly and handsome. I thought his eye took me in, but could not meet it. This procession went by to a door in the close, which a serving-man in fine livery set open; and two of the soldier-lads carried the prisoner within, the rest lingering with their firelocks by the door.

There can nothing pass in the streets of a city without some following of idle folk and children. It was so now; but the more part melted away incontinent until but three were left. One was a girl; she was dressed like a lady, and had a screen of the Drummond colours on her head; but her comrades or (should I say) followers were ragged gillies, such as I had seen the matches of by the dozen in my Highland journey. They all spoke together earnestly in Gaelic, the sound of which was pleasant in my ears for the sake of Alan; and though the rain was by again, and my porter plucked at me to be going, I even drew nearer where they were, to listen. The lady scolded sharply, the others making apologies and cringeing before her, so that I made sure she was come of a chief's house. All the while the three of them sought in their pockets, and by what I could make out, they had the matter of half a farthing among the party; which made me smile a little to see all Highland folk alike for fine obeisances and empty sporrans.

It chanced the girl turned suddenly about, so that I saw her face for the first time. There is no greater wonder than the way the face of a young woman fits in a man's mind, and stays there, and he could never tell you why; it just seems it was the thing he wanted. She had wonderful bright eyes like stars, and I daresay the eyes had a part in it; but what I remember the most clearly was the way her lips were a trifle open as she turned. And whatever was the cause, I stood there staring like a fool. On her side, as she had not known there was anyone so near, she looked at me a little longer, and perhaps with more surprise, than was entirely civil.

It went through my country head she might be wondering at my new clothes; with that, I blushed to my hair, and at the sight of my colouring it is to be supposed she drew her own conclusions, for she moved her gillies farther down the close, and they fell again to this dispute where I could hear no more of it.

GOSFORD'S CLOSE

PLATE 6

The events of Catriona *take place in 1751, but buildings in
Gosford Close, which was pulled down in 1835, went back to
before the Reformation and are typical of Stevenson's description.*

ANECDOTES AND EGOTISMS

HENRY MACKENZIE

THE LAWN MERCAT was the chief quarter for persons of distinction. It used to be a sort of sight to go to a window there and see the ladies walking (which they always did in fair weather) along that street to the tea-parties at five in the afternoon. Dr Munro the first of that name, one of the founders, it may be said, of the Medical School of Edinburgh, had a house there. I remember a droll circumstance about him. He had a favourite parrot, which spoke with great fluency and distinctness, and which hung at one of his windows, and was a great amusement to the walkers in the Lawn Mercat. The Doctor was called to some distant patient, and remained absent for some weeks. The Doctor was a zealous Whig; his wife, a daughter of the McDonald family, was a not less keen Jacobite. The Doctor had taught the bird the loyal song of *God Save the King*, which was not quite agreeable to the ears of Mrs Munro. During the Doctor's absence, when the bird began to sing that song, she always silenced him with a 'Hush, you rogue!' On the Doctor's return, he was surprised at the silence of the bird who never sung the loyal song. The Doctor begun it himself, when the bird instantly rebuked him with the words, 'Hush, you rogue!'

LAWNMARKET AND THE HEAD OF THE WEST BOW FROM THE WEST

PLATE 7

*The table of books outside the building belongs to Thomas
Nelson, founder of the publishing firm which still bears his name,
who set up shop there in 1798.*

THE YOUNG LAIRD AND EDINBURGH KATY

Allan Ramsay

NOW wat ye wha I met yestreen,
  Coming down the street, my jo?
My mistress, in her tartan screen,
  Fou' bonny, braw, and sweet my jo.
My dear, (quoth I,) thanks to the night,
  That never wish'd a lover ill;
Since ye're out of your mother's sight,
  Let's tak a wauk up to the hill.

O Katy! wiltu gang wi' me,
  And leave the dinsome town a while?
The blossom's sprouting frae the tree,
  And a' the simmer's gawn to smile;
The mavis, nightingale, and lark,
  The bleeting lambs and whistling hynd,
In ilka dale, green, shaw, and park,
  Will nourish health, and glad ye'r mind.

Soon as the clear goodman of day
  Does bend his morning draught of dew,
We'll gae to some burnside and play,
  And gather flow'rs to busk ye'r brow.
We'll pou the daisies on the green,
  The lucken gowans frae the bog;
Between hands now and then we'll lean,
  And sport upo' the velvet fog.

There's up into a pleasant glen,
  A wee piece frae my father's tower,
A canny, saft, and flow'ry den,
  Which circling birks has form'd bower:
Whene'er the sun grows high and warm,
  We'll to the cawler shade remove;
There will I lock thee in mine arm,
  And love and kiss, and kiss and love.

24

CASTLEHILL

PLATE 8

Looking back up the street from the shop in plate 7. The original drawing for this engraving was done between 1840, when Thomas Nelson moved his premises across the way (his name can be seen partly hidden by the lamp over the door of the end building on the right) and 1845, when the whole row was razed. However all the buildings on the right were in existence in Ramsay's time.

PETER'S LETTERS TO HIS KINSFOLK

JOHN GIBSON LOCKHART

THE COURTS of justice with which all these eminent men are so closely connected, are placed in and about the same range of buildings, which in former times were set apart for the accommodation of the Parliament of Scotland.[1] The main approach to these buildings lies through a small oblong square which takes from this circumstance the name of 'the Parliament Close.' On two sides this Close is surrounded by houses of the same gigantic kind of elevation which I have already described to you, and in these, of old, were lodged a great proportion of the dignitaries and principal practitioners of the adjacent courts. At present, however, they are dedicated, like most of the houses in the same quarter of the city, to the accommodation of the tradespeople, and the inferior persons attached to the Courts of Law. The western side of the quadrangle is occupied in all its length by the Church of St Giles's, which in the later times of Scottish Episcopacy possessed the dignity of a Cathedral, and which, indeed, has been the scene of many of the most remarkable incidents in the ecclesiastical history of Scotland. In its general exterior, this church presents by no means a fine specimen of the Gothic architecture, although there are several individual parts about the structure which display great beauty—the tower above all

which rises out of the centre of the pile, and is capped with a very rich and splendid canopy in the shape of a Crown Imperial. This beautiful tower and canopy form a fine point in almost every view of the city of Edinburgh; but the effect of the whole building, when one hears and thinks of it as a Cathedral, is a thing of no great significance. The neighbourhood of the Castle would indeed take something from the impression produced by the greatest Cathedral I am acquainted with, were it placed on the site of St Giles's; but nothing assuredly could have formed a finer accompaniment of softening and soothing interest to the haughty and imperious sway of that majestic fortress, than some large reposing mass of religious architecture, lifting itself as if under its protection out of the heart of the city which it commands. The only want, if want there be, in the whole aspect of this city, is, that of some such type of the grandeur of Religion rearing itself in the air, in somewhat of its due proportion of magnitude and magnificence. It is the only great city, the first impression of whose greatness is not blended with ideas suggested by the presence of some such edifice, piercing the sky in splendour or in gloom, far above the frailer and lowlier habitations of those that come to worship beneath its roof.

[1] See plate 10

ST GILES' CHURCH FROM HIGH STREET

PLATE 9

*As it was between 1817 when the Luckenbooths, the row of shops
and apartments attached to the end of the Tolbooth, were
demolished, and 1827, when this front of the church was altered.
Lockhart's book was published in 1819.*

LIFE OF PERCY BYSSHE SHELLEY

THOMAS JEFFERSON HOGG

SHELLEY and his future bride had travelled from London to Edinburgh by the mail without stopping. A young Scotch advocate was their companion in the coach for part of the way; he was an agreeable, obliging person. Shelley confided to him the object of his journey, and asked his advice.

The young lawyer told the young poet how to get married. They followed his directions and were married on their arrival in Edinburgh—how, or where, I never heard. Harriet had some marriage lines, which she sent to her father. I never saw them.

This young man lived in Edinburgh with his family, but at that time they were all in the country: he was alone in the empty house; he expressed much regret that it was not in his power, therefore, to show the bride and groom hospitality. Shelley saw him several times afterwards; I never did.

I was curious to see something of the courts of justice; I told Bysshe to ask his friend how this could be effected.

His answer was: 'It was impossible; it was vacation, and all the courts were closed.'

Being one day alone in the Parliament Close, I observed that the Parliament House was open. I entered it as others did. I saw one very old man on the bench; his head was shaking, and he shook the papers, which he held in his trembling hands; with a feeble, broken, quivering voice, he was prattling something in broad Scotch. Very few persons were present. It was interlocutory, they said—merely interlocutory.

I asked a man, who appeared to be an usher or doorkeeper, who the judge was.

'Oh! he is an old man; a poor old creature; a poor, wretched old creature; a miserable old creature!'

In England, such an answer, spoken aloud, would have appeared indecorous; but we were a less wise—a less civilized—people. Probably the superannuated Rhadamanthus was deaf as well as feeble, for he heeded it not. I still persisted in asking his name.

'It is just the Lord Ordinary.'

'But what is his name?'

'It is just the Lord Ordinary. He will have a name. It is very like—oh! he will have a name! It is very like, indeed—but I do not rightly ken what it is. I dare say he will have a name. It is just the Lord Ordinary—poor old creature!' And in this the bystanders unanimously concurred.

PARLIAMENT HOUSE 1819

PLATE 10

*The building was finished in 1639 and served the Scottish
Parliament until the Union in 1707, when it became law courts.
The frontage was redesigned in 1810, the year before Shelley's
trip to Edinburgh. The equestrian statue of Charles II was cast
in 1685.*

THE EXPEDITION OF HUMPHREY CLINKER

Tobias Smollett

THE CITY stands upon two hills, and the bottom between them; and, with all its defects, may very well pass for the capital of a moderate kingdom. It is full of people, and continually resounds with the noise of coaches and other carriages, for luxury as well as commerce. As far as I can perceive, here is no want of provisions. The beef and mutton are as delicate here as in Wales; the sea affords plenty of good fish; the bread is remarkably fine; and the water is excellent, though I'm afraid not in sufficient quantity to answer all the purposes of cleanliness and convenience; articles in which, it must be allowed, our fellow-subjects are a little defective. The water is brought in leaden pipes from a mountain in the neighbourhood, to a cistern on Castlehill, from whence it is distributed to public conduits in different parts of the city. From these it is carried in barrels, on the backs of male and female porters, up two, three, four, five, six, seven, and eight pair of stairs, for the use of particular families. Every story is a complete house, occupied by a separate family; and the stair being common to them all, is generally left in a very filthy condition; a man must tread with great circumspection to get safe housed with unpolluted shoes. Nothing can form a stronger contrast, than the difference betwixt the outside and inside of the door; for the good women of this metropolis are remarkably nice in the ornaments and propriety of their apartments, as if they were resolved to transfer the imputation from the individual to the public. You are no stranger to their method of discharging all their impurities from their windows at a certain hour of the night, as the custom is in Spain, Portugal, and some parts of France and Italy—a practice to which I can by no means be reconciled; for notwithstanding all the care that is taken by their scavengers to remove this nuisance every morning by break of day, enough still remains to offend the eyes, as well as other organs of those whom use has not hardened against all delicacy of sensation. . . .

As to the surprising height of their houses, it is absurd in many respects; but in one particular light I cannot view it without horror; that is, the dreadful situation of all the families above, in case the common stair-case should be rendered impassable by a fire in the lower stories. In order to prevent the shocking consequences that must attend such an accident, it would be a right measure to open doors of communication from one house to another, on every story, by which the people might fly from such a terrible visitation. In all parts of the world, we see the force of habit prevailing over all the dictates of convenience and sagacity. All the people of business at Edinburgh, and even the genteel company, may be seen standing in crowds every day, from one to two in the afternoon, in the open street, at a place where formerly stood a market-cross, which (by the bye) was a curious piece of Gothic architecture, still to be seen in Lord Somerville's garden in this neighbourhood. I say, the people stand in the open street from the force of custom, rather than move a few yards to an exchange that stands empty on one side, or to the Parliament-close on the other, which is a noble square, adorned with a fine equestrian statue of king Charles II.

ROYAL EXCHANGE

PLATE 11

The building was finished in 1761, nine years before the publication of Smollett's novel. However the merchants continued to prefer to do their business in the street and the building became, as it still is today, the municipal offices. A 'conduit' can be seen in plate 15. The Mercat, or Market, Cross (see title page drawing for the form in which it was rebuilt in 1617) was taken down in 1756 because it was felt that its appearance would shame the Royal Exchange, and removed by Lord Somerville to his Estate. It was replaced in 1785 by a pillar designated the Mercat Cross, which was moved to its present position in 1885.

FROM

ANECDOTES AND EGOTISMS

HENRY MACKENZIE

GOLF, a favourite amusement of Edinburgh, was played on Bruntsfield Links, tho' the crack players preferred those of Leith. I recollect a wager laid by a celebrated golfer, that he could strike a ball from one of the windows in the building at the end of the Luckenbooths looking down the street, in six strokes to the top of Arthur's Seat, the first stroke to be from the bottom of a stone basin. He won his bet; the first stroke striking the ball to the Cross, and the second reaching the middle of the Canongate.

HIGH STREET

PLATE 12

*The colonnade on the left marks the entrance to the Royal
Exchange: the tower on the right-hand side of the street is Tron
Church. Beyond is Canongate. This is exactly the prospect the
golfer would have faced when addressing his second shot. See
plate 54 for Bruntsfield Links.*

OUR STREET

Josiah Livingstone

><:

THE DEACON had many stories to tell of the actings of the Council in his own day. How the bell rope at the Town Guard-house broke, and they required three meetings and three suppers to settle what length should be chain and what length rope. How after one of these sederunts in 'John's' Coffee-house, as they came down the High Street to the Tron Church, the moon shone brightly and the Tron Church appeared to be greatly off the perpendicular. How the Deacons, invested with the cares of office, saw it to be their duty to give the church a hearty shove to make it right; for which end they took off their coats and laid them down, and applied their shoulders with right good will, always retiring a little now and then to see what the effect was. How, after a while they thought the mischief was mended, and that they might put on their coats. But some thief had meantime walked off with these, and they could not be found, but how the Deacon of the Glovers, old Mr Gladow, explained it in a moment, 'Eh, sirs, but ou've shoved weel, ou've covered our coats.'

TRADITIONS OF EDINBURGH

Robert Chambers

IT IS HARDLY surprising that habits carried to such an extravagance amongst gentlemen should have in some small degree affected the fairer and purer of heart of creation also. It is an old story in Edinburgh that three ladies had one night a merry-meeting in a tavern near the Cross, where they sat till a very late hour. Ascending at length to the street, they scarcely remembered where they were; but as it was good moonlight, they found little difficulty in walking along till they came to the Tron Church. Here, however, an obstacle occurred. The moon, shining high in the south, threw the shadow of the steeple directly across the street from the one side to the other; and the ladies, being no more clear-sighted than they were clear-headed, mistook this for a broad and rapid river, which they would be required to cross before making further way. In this delusion, they sat down upon the brink of the imaginary stream, deliberately took off their shoes and stockings, kilted their lower garments, and proceeded to wade through to the opposite side; after which, resuming their shoes and stockings, they went on their way rejoicing, as before!

TRON CHURCH

PLATE 13

Founded in 1637 by order of Charles I. The original wooden spire illustrated here was burned down in the fire of 1824 and replaced by the present one in stone. The church has been out of use since 1952.

MY SCHOOLS AND SCHOOLMASTERS

Hugh Miller

THE GREAT FIRES of the Parliament Close and the High Street were events of this winter. A countryman, who had left town when the old spire of the Tron Church was blazing like a torch, and the large group of buildings nearly opposite the Cross still enveloped in flame from ground-floor to roof-tree, passed our work-shed, a little after two o'clock, and, telling us what he had seen, remarked that, if the conflagration went on as it was doing, we would have, as our next season's employment, the Old Town of Edinburgh to rebuild. And as the evening closed over our labours, we went in to town in a body to see the fires that promised to do so much for us. The spire had burnt out, and we could but catch between us and the darkened sky the square abrupt outline of the masonry a-top that had supported the wooden broach, whence, only a few hours before, Fergusson's bell had descended in a molten shower. The flames, too, in the upper group of buildings, were restricted to the lower stories and flared fitfully on the tall forms and bright swords of the dragoons, drawn from the neighbouring barracks, as they rode up and down the middle space, or gleamed athwart the street on groups of wretched-looking women and ruffian men, who seemed scanning with greedy eyes the still unremoved heaps of household goods rescued from the burning tenements. The first figure that caught my eye was a singularly ludicrous one. Removed from the burning mass but by the thickness of a wall, there was a barber's shop brilliantly lighted with gas, the uncurtained window of which permitted the spectators outside to see whatever was going on in the interior. The barber was as busily at work as if he were a hundred miles from the scene of danger, though the engines at the time were playing against the outside of his gable wall; and the immediate subject under his hands, as my eye rested upon him, was an immensely fat old fellow, on whose round bald forehead and ruddy cheeks the perspiration, occasioned by the oven-like heat of the place, was standing out in huge drops, and whose vast mouth, widely open to accommodate the man of the razor, gave to his countenance such an expression as I have sometimes seen in grotesque Gothic heads of that age of art in which the ecclesiastical architect began to make sport of his religion. . . . Nearly two hundred families were already at this time cast homeless into the streets. Shortly before quitting the scene of the conflagration for the country, I passed along a common stair, which led from the Parliament Close towards the Cowgate, through a tall old domicile, eleven stories in height, and I afterwards remembered that the passage was occupied by a smouldering oppressive vapour, which, from the direction of the wind, could scarce have been derived from the adjacent conflagration, though at the time, without thinking much of the circumstance, I concluded it might have come creeping westwards on some low cross current along the narrow lanes. In less than an hour after that lofty tenement was wrapt in flames, from the ground story to more than a hundred feet over its tallest chimneys, and about sixty additional families, its tenants, were cast into the streets with the others.

PARLIAMENT HOUSE FROM COWGATE

PLATE 14

Drawn in 1819, this is almost certainly the 'common stair . . . from Parliament Close towards the Cowgate' to which Miller refers in his account of the fire in 1824 (see also page 35).

Miller's memory may have been at fault over the height of the adjacent buildings but the fact remains that some tenements in that area were as many as fifteen stories high.

THE JOURNAL OF A TOUR TO THE HEBRIDES

James Boswell

I AM, I flatter myself, completely a citizen of the world.— In my travels through Holland, Germany, Switzerland, Italy, Corsica, France, I never felt myself from home; and I sincerely love 'every kindred and tongue and people and nation'. I subscribe to what my late truly learned and philosophical friend Mr Crosbie said, that the English are better animals than the Scots; they are nearer the sun; their blood is richer, and more mellow: but when I humour any of them in an outrageous contempt of Scotland, I fairly own I treat them as children. And thus I have, at some moments, found myself obliged to treat even Dr Johnson.

To Scotland however he ventured; and he returned from it in great good humour, with his prejudices much lessened, and with very grateful feelings of the hospitality with which he was treated; as is evident from that admirable work, his *Journey to the Western Islands of Scotland*, which, to my utter astonishment, has been misapprehended, even to rancour, by many of my countrymen.

To have the company of Chambers and Scott, he delayed his journey so long, that the court of session, which rises on the eleventh of August, was broke up before he got to Edinburgh.

On Saturday the fourteenth of August, 1773, late in the evening, I received a note from him, that he was arrived at Boyd's inn, at the head of the Canongate. I went to him directly. He embraced me cordially; and I exulted in the thought, that I now had him actually in Caledonia. Mr Scott's amiable manners, and attachment to our *Socrates*, at once united me to him. He told me that, before I came in, the Doctor had unluckily had a bad specimen of Scottish cleanliness. He then drank no fermented liquor. He asked to have his lemonade made sweeter; upon which the waiter, with his greasy fingers, lifted a lump of sugar, and put it into it. The Doctor, in indignation, threw it out of the window. Scott said, he was afraid he would have knocked the waiter down. Dr Johnson and I walked arm-in-arm up the High-street, to my house in James's court: it was a dusky night: I could not prevent his being assailed by the evening effluvia of Edinburgh. I heard a late baronet, of some distinction in the political world in the beginning of the present reign, observe, that 'walking the streets of Edinburgh at night was pretty perilous, and a good deal odoriferous.' The peril is much abated, by the care which the magistrates have taken to enforce the city laws against throwing foul water from the windows; but, from the structure of the houses in the old town, which consist of many stories, in each of which a different family lives, and there being no covered sewers, the odour still continues. A zealous Scotsman would have wished Dr Johnson to be without one of his five senses upon this occasion. As we marched slowly along, he grumbled in my ear, 'I smell you in the dark!' But he acknowledged that the breadth of the street, and the loftiness of the buildings on each side, made a noble appearance.

HIGH STREET AND THE HEAD OF CANONGATE

PLATE 15

The White Horse Inn, kept at that time by a man named Boyd, was in St Mary's Wynd (now Street) which ran off to the right and was then just outside the city boundary. James' Court is at the bottom of Castlehill just below and on the same side of the street as the row of houses in plate 7. Almost immediately after they turned into High Street Johnson and Boswell would have passed John Knox's House (left of the picture) and the public well (one of Smollett's 'conduits'— see page 30) which stands below its bow window.

ANNALS OF THE PARISH

JOHN GALT

I WAS named in this year for the General Assembly, and Mrs Balwhidder by her continual thrift having made our purse able to stand a shake against the wind, we resolved to go into Edinburgh in a creditable manner. Accordingly, in conjunct with Mrs Dalrymple, the lady of a major of that name, we hired the Irville chaise, and we put up in Glasgow at the Black Boy, where we stayed all night. Next morning, by seven o'clock, we got into the fly-coach for the capital of Scotland, which we reached after a heavy journey about the same hour in the evening. We put up at the public where it stopped till the next day, for really both me and Mrs Balwhidder were worn out with the undertaking, and found a cup of tea a vast refreshment.

Betimes in the morning, having taken our breakfast, we got a caddy to guide us and our wallise to Widow M'Vicar's, at the head of the Covenanters' Close. She was a relation to my first wife, Betty Lanshaw, my own full cousin that was, and we had advised her, by course of post, of our coming and intendment to lodge with her as uncos and strangers. But Mrs M'Vicar kept a cloth shop, and sold plaidings and flannels, besides Yorkshire superfines, and was used to the sudden incoming of strangers, especially visitants, from both the West and the North Highlands, and was withal a gawsy, furthy woman, taking great pleasure in hospitality, and every sort of kindliness and discretion; and she would not allow of such a thing as our being lodgers in her house, but was so cagey to see us, and to have it in her power to be civil to a minister (as she was pleased to say) of such repute, that nothing less would content her but that we must live upon her, and partake of all the best that could be gotten for us within the walls of 'the gude town.'

When we found ourselves so comfortable, Mrs Balwhidder and me waited on my patron's family that was, the young ladies, and the laird, who had been my pupil, but was now an advocate high in the law. They likewise were kind. In short, everybody in Edinburgh was in a manner wearisome kind, and we could scarcely find time to see the Castle and the palace of Holyrood House, and that more sanctified place where the Maccabeus of the Kirk of Scotland, John Knox, was wont to live.

JOHN KNOX'S HOUSE

PLATE 16

Tradition has it that the house was originally built in about 1490, that John Knox lived in it, or a part of it, from 1561 to 1572, and that at some earlier date it was occupied by George Durie, Abbot of Dunfermline, who was later canonised. It certainly belonged to James Mossman, goldsmith to Mary Queen of Scots. Last restored in 1958, it is kept as a museum of Knox and the Scottish Reformation. This engraving was published in 1820, when Galt would have been writing Annals of the Parish.

A HISTORY OF THE REBELLION OF 1745

JOHN HOME

ABOUT TEN O'CLOCK that night, the deputies returned, and brought a letter in answer to the message sent by them.

His Royal Highness the Prince Regent thinks his Manifesto, and the King his father's declaration already published, a sufficient capitulation for all His Majesty's subjects to accept of with joy. His present demands are to be received into the city as the son and representative of the King his father, and obeyed as such when there. His Royal Highness supposes, that since the receipt of his letter to the Provost, no arms or ammunition have been suffered to be carried off or concealed, and will expect a particular account of all things of that nature. Lastly, he expects a positive answer before two o'clock in the morning, otherwise he well think himself obliged to take measures conform.

At Gray's Mill, 16th September, 1745.
By His Highness's command.
(Signed)   J. MURRAY

When this letter was read, Provost Stuart said, there was one condition in it which he would die rather than submit to, which was receiving the son of the Pretender as Prince Regent; for he was bound by oath to another master. After long deliberation it was determined to send out deputies once more in the morning, that the Magistrates might have an opportunity of conversing with the citizens, most of whom were gone to bed. The deputies were also instructed to require an explanation of what was meant by receiving Charles as Prince Regent.

About two o'clock in the morning the deputies set out in a hackney coach for Gray's Mill; when they arrived there they prevailed upon Lord George Murray to second their application for a delay; but Charles refused to grant it; and the deputies were ordered in his name to get them gone.

The coach brought them back to Edinburgh, set them down in the High Street, and then drove towards the Canongate. When the Nether Bow port was opened to let out the coach, 800 Highlanders, led by Cameron of Lochiel, rushed in, and took possession of the city.

It was about five o'clock in the morning when the rebels entered Edinburgh. They immediately sent parties to all the other gates, and to the town guard, who making the soldiers upon duty prisoners, occupied their posts as quietly as one guard relieves another. When the inhabitants of Edinburgh awaked in the morning, they found that the Highlanders were masters of the city.

NETHERBOW PORT FROM THE EAST

PLATE 17

The building was taken down in 1764. Brass plaques in the road today mark its site and also the point at which until 1856 the separate burgh of Canongate began.

FROM

TOUR THROUGH THE WHOLE ISLAND

DANIEL DEFOE

THE CHURCHES in this populous city are but ten, (viz.) 1. The Cannon-gate Church 2. The College Kirk[1] 3. The Trone Kirk[2] 4. The New Kirk 5. The Old Kirk 6. The Tolbrook Kirk 7. The Haddocks Hole Kirk[3] 8. The Lady Yester's Kirk 9. The Gray Friars Kirk[4] 10. The West Kirk.[5]

There are also many meeting-houses of the Episcopal party who call themselves Church of England, though they do not all use the English Common-Prayer. These are the dissenters in Scotland, as the Presbyterians are Dissenters in England.

There are also two churches at Leith, and very large and very full they are, and so indeed are all the churches in the city, for the people of Scotland do not wander about on the sabbath-days, as in England; and even those who may have no more religion than enough, yet custom has made it almost natural to them, they all go to the kirk.

They have also one very good custom as to their behaviour in the church, which I wish were practis'd here, namely, that after the sermon is over, and the blessing given, they all look round upon their friends, and especially to persons of distinction, and make their civilities and bows as we do here, for, by the way, the Scots do not want manners. But if any person come in when the worship is begun, he takes no notice of no body, not any body of him; whereas here we make our bows and our cringes in the middle of our very prayers. . . .

The palace is a handsome building, rather convenient than large. The entrance is majestick, and over the gate a large apartment, which the Duke of Hamilton claims as housekeeper, or rather gate-keeper of the palace; within this is a large, irregular court, where, I must needs say, are very improperly plac'd the coach-houses and stables, which should much rather have been farther off, either in the park, or without the outgate: And, if here had been a barrack, or guard-house, like the Horse-Guards at Whitehall, it would have look'd more like a royal palace for the king. On either side of this court are gardens, yards the Scots call them, whereof one is like our apothecaries garden at Chelsea, call'd a physick garden, and is tolerably well stor'd with simples, and some exoticks of value; and, particularly as I was told, there was a rhubarb-tree, or plant, and which throve very well.[6]

[1] Trinity College Church, see plate 38.

[2] See plate 13.

[3] The New Kirk, Old Kirk, Tolbrook (Tolbooth) Kirk and Haddocks (Haddo's) Hole Kirk were separate churches within St Giles'.

[4] See plate 27.

[5] An older church on the site of St Cuthbert's Church, pulled down in 1775. See frontispiece illustration.

[6] While the forerunner of the Royal Botanic Garden was established in the grounds of Holyrood Palace, it had been moved in 1676 to a site attached to Trinity College, where Waverley Station now stands.

CANONGATE CHURCH

PLATE 18

Built in about 1690, some thirty years before Defoe's visit.
Robert Fergusson is buried in the churchyard.

THE EXECUTION OF MONTROSE

William Edmonstoune Aytoun

COME hither, Evan Cameron!
  Come, stand beside my knee—
I hear the river roaring down
  Towards the wintry sea.
There's shouting on the mountain-side,
  There's war within the blast—
Old faces look upon me,
  Old forms go trooping past:
I hear the pibroch wailing
  Amidst the din of fight,
And my dim spirit wakes again
  Upon the verge of night.

'Twas I that led the Highland host
  Through wild Lochaber's snows,
What time the plaided clans came down
  To battle with Montrose.
I've told thee how the Southrons fell
  Beneath the broad claymore,
And how we smote the Campbell clan
  By Inverlochy's shore.
I've told thee how we swept Dundee,
  And tamed the Lindsay's pride;
But never have I told thee yet
  How the great Marquis died.

A traitor sold him to his foes;
  O deed of deathless shame!
I charge thee, boy, if e'er thou meet
  With one of Assynt's name—
Be it upon the mountain's side,
  Or yet within the glen,
Stand he in martial gear alone,
  Or backed by armèd men—
Face him, as thou wouldst face the man
  Who wronged thy sire's renown;
Remember of what blood thou art,
  And strike the caitiff down!

They brought him to the Watergate,
  Hard bound with hempen span,
As though they held a lion there,
  And not a fenceless man.
They set him high upon a cart—
  The hangman rode below—
They drew his hands behind his back,
  And bared his noble brow.
Then, as a hound is slipped from leash,
  They cheered the common throng,
And blew the note with yell and shout,
  And bade him pass along.

It would have made a brave man's heart
  Grow sad and sick that day,
To watch the keen malignant eyes
  Bent down on that array.
There stood the Whig west-country lords,
  In balcony and bow;
There sat their gaunt and withered dames,
  And their daughters all a-row.
And every open window
  Was full as full might be
With black-robed Covenanting carles,
  That goodly sport to see!

But when he came, though pale and wan,
  He looked so great and high,
So noble was his manly front,
  So calm his steadfast eye;—
The rabble rout forbore to shout,
  And each man held his breath,
For well they knew the hero's soul
  Was face to face with death.
And then a mournful shudder
  Through all the people crept,
And some that came to scoff at him
  Now turned aside and wept.

THE WATERGATE

PLATE 19

*As it was in the time of Aytoun. The ornamental arch blew down
in 1822, but had to be replaced because in its absence the
fishwives of Newhaven and Musselburgh refused to pay duty on
the loads they brought in. It was finally removed around the time
when this poem was first published, which was in 1844.*

But onwards—always onwards,
  In silence and in gloom,
The dreary pageant laboured,
  Till it reached the house of doom.
Then first a woman's voice was heard
  In jeer and laughter loud,
And an angry cry and a hiss arose
  From the heart of the tossing crowd:
Then as the Graeme looked upwards,
  He saw the ugly smile
Of him who sold his king for gold—
  The master-fiend Argyle!

The Marquis gazed a moment,
  And nothing did he say,
But the cheek of Argyle grew ghastly pale,
  And he turned his eyes away.
The painted harlot by his side,
  She shook through every limb,
For a roar like thunder swept the street,
  And hands were clenched at him;
And a Saxon soldier cried aloud,
  'Back, coward, from thy place!
For seven long years thou hast not dared
  To look him in the face.'

Had I been there with sword in hand,
  And fifty Camerons by,
That day through high Dunedin's streets
  Had pealed the slogan-cry.
Not all their troops of trampling horse,
  Nor might of mailèd men—
Not all the rebels in the south
  Had borne us backwards then!
Once more his foot on Highland heath
  Had trod as free as air,
Or I, and all who bore my name,
  Been laid around him there!

It might not be. They placed him next
  Within the solemn hall,
Where once the Scottish kings were throned
  Amidst their nobles all.
But there was dust of vulgar feet
  On that polluted floor,
And perjured traitors filled the place
  Where good men sate before.
With savage glee came Warristoun
  To read the murderous doom;
And then uprose the great Montrose
  In the middle of the room.

'Now, by my faith as belted knight,
  And by the name I bear,
And by the bright Saint Andrew's cross
  That waves above us there—
Yea, by a greater, mightier oath—
  And oh, that such should be!—
By that dark stream of royal blood
  That lies 'twixt you and me—
I have not sought in battle-field
  A wreath of such renown,
Nor dared I hope on my dying day
  To win the martyr's crown!

'There is a chamber far away
  Where sleep the good and brave,
But a better place ye have named for me
  Than by my father's grave.
For truth and right, 'gainst treason's might,
  This hand hath always striven,
And ye raise it up for a witness still
  In the eye of earth and heaven.
Then nail my head on yonder tower—
  Give every town a limb—
And God who made shall gather them;
  I go from you to Him!'

REGENT MURRAY'S HOUSE 1820

PLATE 20

*Built in about 1630 and now part of Moray House College of
Education. It is said that from this balcony Argyle and his son's
wedding-party looked down on Montrose as he was taken up
Canongate bound to a seat on the hangman's cart.*

The morning dawned full darkly,
  The rain came flashing down,
And the jagged streak of the levin-bolt
  Lit up the gloomy town:
The thunder crashed across the heaven,
  The fatal hour was come:
Yet aye broke in with muffled beat,
  The 'larum of the drum.
There was madness on the earth below
  And anger in the sky,
And young and old, and rich and poor,
  Came forth to see him die.

Ah, God! that ghastly gibbet!
  How dismal 'tis to see
The great tall spectral skeleton,
  The ladder and the tree!
Hark! hark! it is the clash of arms—
  The bells begin to toll—
'He is coming! he is coming!
  God's mercy on his soul!'
One last long peal of thunder—
  The clouds are cleared away,
And the glorious sun once more looks down
  Amidst the dazzling day.

'He is coming! he is coming!'
  Like a bridegroom from his room,
Came the hero from his prison
  To the scaffold and the doom.
There was glory on his forehead,
  There was lustre in his eye,
And he never walked to battle
  More proudly than to die:
There was colour in his visage,
  Though the cheeks of all were wan,
And they marvelled as they saw him pass,
  That great and goodly man!

He mounted up the scaffold,
  And he turned him to the crowd;
But they dared not trust the people,
  So he might speak aloud.
But he looked upon the heavens,
  And they were clear and blue,
And in the liquid ether
  The eye of God shone through!
Yet a black and murky battlement
  Lay resting on the hill,
As though the thunder slept within—
  All else was calm and still.

The grim Geneva ministers
  With anxious scowl drew near,
As you have seen the ravens flock
  Around the dying deer.
He would not deign them word nor sign,
  But alone he bent the knee;
And veiled his face for Christ's dear grace
  Beneath the gallows-tree.
Then radiant and serene he rose,
  And cast his cloak away:
For he had ta'en his latest look
  Of earth and sun and day.

A beam of light fell o'er him,
  Like a glory round the shriven,
And he climbed the lofty ladder
  As it were the path to heaven.
Then came a flash from out the cloud,
  And a stunning thunder-roll;
And no man dared to look aloft,
  For fear was on every soul.
There was another heavy sound,
  A hush and then a groan;
And darkness swept across the sky—
  The work of death was done!

THE TOLBOOTH FROM THE SOUTH WEST

PLATE 21

After sentence in Parliament House (see page 58) Montrose was lodged for the night in the Tolbooth. He was hanged at the Mercat Cross (see title page) on a scaffold 30 feet high, and his head stuck on a spike high up on the west face of the Tolbooth. It is said that it stayed there for eleven years, after which it was removed to make room for the head of Argyle. The Tolbooth itself was taken down in 1817 (see also page 90).

THE HEART OF MIDLOTHIAN

THAT TUMULT was now transferred from the inside to the outside of the Tolbooth. The mob had brought their destined victim forth, and were about to conduct him to the common place of execution, which they had fixed as the scene of his death. The leader, whom they distinguished by the name of Madge Wildfire, had been summoned to assist at the procession by the impatient shouts of his confederates.

'I will ensure you five hundred pounds,' said the unhappy man, grasping Wildfire's hand,—'five hundred pounds for to save my life.'

The other answered in the same undertone, and returning his grasp with one equally convulsive, 'Five hundred-weight of coined gold should not save you.—Remember Wilson!'

A deep pause of a minute ensued, when Wildfire added in a more composed tone, 'Make your peace with Heaven.—Where is the clergyman?'

Butler, who, in great terror and anxiety, had been detained within a few yards of the Tolbooth door, to wait the event of the search after Porteous, was now brought forward, and commanded to walk by the prisoner's side, and to prepare him for immediate death. His answer was a supplication that the rioters would consider what they did. 'You are neither judges nor jury,' said he. 'You cannot have, by the laws of God or man, power to take away the life of a human creature, however deserving he may be of death. If it is murder even in a lawful magistrate to execute an offender otherwise than in the place, time, and manner which the judges' sentence prescribes, what must it be in you, who have no warrant for interference but your own wills? In the name of Him who is all mercy, show mercy to this unhappy man, and do not dip your hands in his blood, nor rush into the very crime which you are desirous of avenging!'

'Cut your sermon short—you are not in your pulpit,' answered one of the rioters.

'If we hear more of your clavers,' said another, 'we are like to hang you up beside him.'

'Peace—hush!' said Wildfire. 'Do the good man no harm—he discharges his conscience, and I like him the better.'

He then addressed Butler. 'Now, sir, we have patiently heard you, and we just wish you to understand, in the way of answer, that you may as well argue to the ashlar-work and iron stanchels of the Tolbooth as think to change our purpose—Blood must have blood. We have sworn to each other by the deepest oaths ever pledged, that Porteous shall die the death he deserves so richly; therefore, speak no more to us, but prepare him for death as well as the briefness of his change will permit.'

They had suffered the unfortunate Porteous to put on his night-gown and slippers, as he had thrown off his coat and shoes, in order to facilitate his attempted escape up the chimney. In this garb he was now mounted on the hands of two of the rioters, clasped together, so as to form what is called in Scotland, 'The King's Cushion'. Butler was placed close to his side, and repeatedly urged to perform a duty always the most painful which can be imposed on a clergyman deserving of the name, and now rendered more so by the peculiar and horrid circumstances of the criminal's case. Porteous at first uttered some supplications for mercy, but when he found there was no chance that these would be attended to, his military education, and the natural stubbornness of his disposition, combined to support his spirits.

LAWNMARKET AND THE HEAD OF THE WEST BOW FROM THE EAST, WITH THE WEIGH HOUSE

PLATE 22

The lynching of Captain Porteous, who had ordered his men to fire on a crowd at an execution, took place in 1736. 'The common place of execution' was the Grassmarket, and to get there from the Tolbooth he would first have been taken along Lawnmarket to the head of the West Bow where, until 1822 (four years after the publication of The Heart of Midlothian*), stood the Weigh House. Compare this view with plate 7, drawn after the removal of the Weigh House.*

'Are you prepared for this dreadful end?' said Butler in a faltering voice. 'Oh turn to Him, in whose eyes time and space have no existence, and to whom a few minutes are as a lifetime, and a lifetime as a minute.'

'I believe I know what you would say,' answered Porteous sullenly. 'I was bred a soldier; if they will murder me without time, let my sins as well as my blood lie at their door.'

'Who was it,' said the stern voice of Wildfire, 'that said to Wilson, at this very spot, when he could not pray, owing to the galling agony of his fetters, that his pains would soon be over?—I say to you to take your own tale home; and if you cannot profit by the good man's lessons, blame not them that are still more merciful to you than you were to others.'

The procession now moved forward with a slow and determined pace. It was enlightened by many blazing links and torches; for the actors of this work were so far from affecting any secrecy on the occasion, that they seemed even to court observation. Their principal leaders kept close to the person of the prisoner, whose pallid yet stubborn features were seen distinctly by the torchlight, as his person was raised considerably above the concourse which thronged about him. Those who bore swords, muskets, and battle-axes, marched on each side, as if forming a regular guard to the procession. The windows, as they went along, were filled with the inhabitants, whose slumbers had been broken by this unusual disturbance. Some of the spectators muttered accents of encouragement; but in general they were so much appalled by a sight so strange and audacious, that they looked on with a sort of stupefied astonishment. No one offered, by act or word, the slightest interruption.

The rioters, on their part, continued to act with the same air of deliberate confidence and security which had marked all their proceedings. When the object of their resentment dropped one of his slippers, they stopped sought for it, and replaced it upon his foot with great deliberation. As they descended the Bow towards the fatal spot where they designed to complete their purpose, it was suggested that there should be a rope kept in readiness. For this purpose the booth of a man who dealt in cordage was forced open, a coil of rope fit for their purpose was selected to serve as a halter, and the dealer next morning found that a guinea had been left on his counter in exchange; so anxious were the perpetrators of this daring action to show that they meditated not the slightest wrong or infraction of law, excepting so far as Porteous was himself concerned.

Leading, or carrying along with them, in this determined and regular manner, the object of their vengeance, they at length reached the place of common execution, the scene of his crime, and destined spot of his sufferings. Several of the rioters (if they should not rather be described as conspirators) endeavoured to remove the stone which filled up the socket in which the end of the fatal tree was sunk when it was erected for its fatal purpose; others sought for the means of constructing a temporary gibbet, the place in which the gallows itself was deposited being reported too secure to be forced without much loss of time. Butler endeavoured to avail himself of the delay afforded by these circumstances, to turn the people from their desperate design. 'For God's sake,' he exclaimed, 'remember it is the image of your Creator which you are about to deface in the person of this unfortunate man! Wretched as he is, and wicked as he

THE WEST BOW

PLATE 23

As it was when The Heart of Midlothian *was written. The Weigh House can be seen at the top.*

may be, he has a share in every promise of Scripture, and you cannot destroy him in impenitence without blotting his name from the Book of Life—Do not destroy soul and body; give time for preparation.'

'What time had they,' returned a stern voice, 'whom he murdered on this very spot?—The laws both of God and man call for his death.'

'But what, my friends,' insisted Butler, with a generous disregard for his own safety—'what hath constituted you his judges?'

'We are not his judges,' replied the same person; 'he has been already judged and condemned by lawful authority. We are those whom Heaven, and our righteous anger, have stirred up to execute judgment, when a corrupt government would have protected a murderer.'

'I am none,' said the unfortunate Porteous; 'that which you charge upon me fell out in self-defence, in the lawful exercise of my duty.'

'Away with him—away with him!' was the general cry. 'Why do you trifle away time in making a gallows?—that dyester's pole is good enough for the homicide.'

The unhappy man was forced to his fate with remorseless rapidity. Butler, separated from him by the press, escaped the last horrors of his struggles. Unnoticed by those who had hitherto detained him as a prisoner, he fled from the fatal spot, without much caring in what direction his course lay. A loud shout proclaimed the stern delight with which the agents of this deed regarded its completion. Butler, then, at the opening into the low street called the Cowgate, cast back a terrified glance, and, by the red and dusky light of the torches, he could discern a figure wavering and struggling as it hung suspended above the heads of the multitude, and could even observe men striking at it with their Lochaber-axes and partisans. The sight was of a nature to double his horror, and to add wings to his flight.

The street down which the fugitive ran opens to one of the eastern ports or gates of the city. Butler did not stop till he reached it, but found it still shut. He waited nearly an hour, walking up and down in inexpressible perturbation of mind. At length he ventured to call out, and rouse the attention of the terrified keepers of the gate, who now found themselves at liberty to resume their office without interruption. Butler requested them to open the gate. They hesitated. He told them his name and occupation.

'He is a preacher,' said one; 'I have heard him preach in Haddo's Hole.'

'A fine preaching has he been at the night,' said another; 'but may least said is sunest mended.'

Opening then the wicket of the main gate, the keepers suffered Butler to depart, who hastened to carry his horror and fear beyond the walls of Edinburgh. His first purpose was, instantly to take the road homeward; but other fears and cares, connected with the news he had learned in that remarkable day, induced him to linger in the neighbourhood of Edinburgh until daybreak. More than one group of persons passed him as he was whileing away the hours of darkness that yet remained, whom, from the stifled tones of their discourse, the unwonted hour when they travelled, and the hasty pace at which they walked, he conjectured to have been engaged in the late fatal transaction.

56

THE HEAD OF COWGATE FROM THE GRASSMARKET

PLATE 24

As Scott would have known it.

BONNY DUNDEE
FROM
(THE DOOM OF DEVORGOIL)
SIR WALTER SCOTT

Parliament House as it was at the time of the Convention in 1689.

TO the Lords of Convention 'twas Claver'se who spoke,
'Ere the King's crown shall fall there are crowns
       to be broke;
So let each Cavalier who loves honour and me,
Come follow the bonnet of Bonny Dundee.
 'Come fill up my cup, come fill up my can,
 Come saddle your horses, and call up your men;
 Come open the West Port and let me gang free,
 And it's room for the bonnet of Bonny Dundee!'

Dundee he is mounted, he rides up the street,
The bells are rung backward, the drums they are beat;
But the Provost, douce man, said, 'Just e'en let him be,
The Gude Town is weel quit of that Deil of Dundee.'
 Come fill up my cup, &c.

As he rode down the sanctified bends of the Bow,
Ilk carline was flyting and shaking her pow;
But the young plants of grace they look'd couthie and slee,
Thinking, 'Luck to thy bonnet, thou Bonny Dundee!'
 Come fill up my cup, &c.

With sour-featured Whigs the Grassmarket was cramm'
As if half the West had set tryst to be hang'd;
There was spite in each look, there was fear in each e'e,
As they watch'd for the bonnets of Bonny Dundee.
 Come fill up my cup, &c.

These cowls of Kilmarnock had spits and had spears,
And lang-hafted gullies to kill Cavaliers;
But they shrunk to close-heads, and the causeway was f
At the toss of the bonnet of Bonny Dundee.
 Come fill up my cup, &c.

58

GRASSMARKET FROM THE WEST PORT

PLATE 25

In fact Viscount Dundee did not 'ride up the street' on this famous occasion, nor 'down . . . the Bow' (see plate 23), nor through the Grassmarket and out by the West Port as Scott suggests. He went in the opposite direction, out through the Netherbow Port (plate 17), turned left along Leith Wynd, and then left again the other side of the Nor' Loch, to come back to the Castle along what is now Princes Street.

He spurred to the foot of the proud Castle rock,
And with the gay Gordon he gallantly spoke;
'Let Mons Meg and her marrows speak twa words or three,
For the love of the bonnet of Bonny Dundee.'
   Come fill up my cup, &c.

The Gordon demands of him which way he goes—
'Where'er shall direct me the shade of Montrose!
Your Grace in short space shall hear tidings of me,
Or that low lies the bonnet of Bonny Dundee.
   Come fill up my cup, &c.

'There are hills beyond Pentland, and lands beyond Forth,
If there's lords in the Lowlands, there's chiefs in the North;
There are wild Duniewassals, three thousand times three,
Will cry *hoigh!* for the bonnet of Bonny Dundee.
   Come fill up my cup, &c.

'There's brass on the target of barken'd bull hide;
There's steel in the scabbard that dangles beside;
The brass shall be burnished, the steel shall flash free,
At a toss of the bonnet of Bonny Dundee.
   Come fill up my cup, &c.

'Away to the hills, to the caves, to the rocks—
Ere I own an usurper, I'll couch with the fox;
And tremble, false Whigs, in the midst of your glee,
You have not seen the last of my bonnet and me!'
   Come fill up my cup, &c.

He waved his proud hand, and the trumpets were blown,
The kettle-drums clash'd, and the horsemen rode on,
Till on Ravelston's cliffs and on Clermiston's lee,
Died away the wild war-notes of Bonny Dundee.
   Come fill up my cup, come fill up my can,
   Come saddle the horses and call up the men,
   Come open your gates, and let me gae free,
   For it's up with the bonnets of Bonny Dundee!

EDINBURGH CASTLE FROM THE WEST

PLATE 26

However, Dundee certainly did stop at 'the foot of the proud Castle rock' and what is more he climbed up its west face, to have words over the Castle wall with the besieged Governor, the Duke of Gordon.

THE GHAISTS

Robert Fergusson

WHARE the braid planes in dowie murmurs wave
Their ancient taps out owre the cauld-clad grave,
Whare Geordie Girdwood, mony a lang-spun day,
Houkit for gentlest banes the humblest clay,
Twa sheeted ghaists, sae grizly and sae wan,
'Mang lanely tombs their douff discourse began.

WATSON

Cauld blaws the nippin North wi' angry seugh,
And showers his hailstanes frae the Castle Cleugh
Owre the Grayfriars, whare, at mirkest hour,
Bogles and spectres wont to tak their tour,
Harlin the pows and shanks to hidden cairns,
Amang the hemlocks wild, and sun-brunt ferns;
But nane the night, save you and I, hae come
Frae the drear mansions o' the midnight tomb.
Now, whan the dawnin's near, whan cock maun craw,
And wi' his angry bougil gar's withdraw,
Ayont the kirk we'll stap, and there tak bield,
While the black hours our nightly freedom yield.

HERIOT

I'm weel content: but, binna cassen down,
Nor trow the cock will ca' ye hame o'er soon;
For, tho' the eastern lift betakens day,
Changing her rokelay black for mantle gray,
Nae weirlike bird our knell of parting rings,
Nor sheds the cauler moisture frae his wings.
Nature has changed her course; the birds o' day
Dosin in silence on the bendin spray,
While howlets round the craigs at noontide flee,
And bluidy hawks sit singin on the tree.
Ah, Caledon! the land I aince held dear;
Sair mane mak I for thy destruction near:
And thou, Edina! aince my dear abode,

Whan royal Jamie sway'd the sov'reign rod,
In thae blest days, weel did I think bestow'd
To blaw thy poortith by wi' heaps o' gowd;
To mak thee sonsy seem wi' mony a gift,
And gar thy stately turrets speel the lift.
In vain did Danish Jones, wi' gimcrack pains,
In Gothic sculpture fret the pliant stanes;
In vain did he affix my statue here,
Brawly to busk wi' flowers ilk coming year.
My towers are sunk; my lands are barren now;
My fame, my honour, like my flowers, maun dow.

WATSON

Sure, Major Weir, or some sic warlock wight,
Has flung beguilin glamour owre your sight;
Or else some kittle cantrip thrown, I ween,
Has bound in mirlygoes my ain twa een:
If ever aught frae sense cou'd be believ'd
(And seenil hae my senses been deceiv'd),
This moment owre the tap o' Adam's tomb,
Fu' easy can I see your chiefest dome.
Nae corbie fleein there, nor croupin craws,
Seem to forspeak the ruin o' thy ha's;
But a' your towers in wonted order stand,
Steeve as the rocks that hem our native land.

HERIOT

Think na I vent my well-a-day in vain;
Kent ye the cause, ye sure wad join my mane.
Black be the day, that e'er to England's ground
Scotland was eikit by the Union's bond!
For monie a menzie o' destructive ills
The country now maun brook frae mortmain bills,
That void our test'ments, and can freely gie
Sic will and scoup to the ordain'd trustee,

HERIOT'S HOSPITAL FROM GREYFRIARS CHURCHYARD

PLATE 27

The occasion of this poem was a proposal that the whole funds of hospitals and similar charities should be vested in government stock at 3%. George Heriot (1563-1624) was goldsmith and banker to James VI. The hospital (or school) he founded was finished in 1660. Greyfriars Churchyard was the scene of the signing of the National Covenant in 1639, and where 1200 Covenanters were incarcerated in 1679.

That he may tir our stateliest riggins bare;
Nor acres, houses, woods, nor fishings spare,
Till he can lend the stoiterin state a lift,
Wi' gowd in gowpins, as a grassum gift;
In lieu o' whilk, we maun be weel content
To tine the capital for *three per cent.;*
A doughty sum indeed; whan, now-a-days,
They raise provisions as the stents they raise;
Yoke hard the poor, and lat the rich chields be
Pamper'd at ease by ithers' industry.

    Hale interest for my fund can scantly now
Cleed a' my callants' backs, and stap their mou'.
How maun their wymes wi' sairest hunger slack,
Their duds in targets flaff upon their back,
Whan they are doom'd to keep a lastin Lent,
Starving for England's weel, at *three per cent.!*

WATSON

Auld Reikie then may bless the gowden times,
Whan honesty and poortith baith are crimes.
She little ken'd, whan you and I endow'd
Our hospitals for back-gaun burghers' gude,
That e'er our siller or our lands shou'd bring
A gude bien livin to a back-gaun king;
Wha, thanks to Ministry! is grown sae wise,
He downa chew the bitter cud o' vice:
For gin, frae Castlehill to Netherbow,
Wad honest houses bawdy-houses grow,
The Crown wad never spier the price o' sin,
Nor hinder younkers to the deil to rin;
But, gif some mortal grien for pious fame,
And leave the poor man's prayer to sane his name,
His gear maun a' be scatter'd by the claws
O' ruthless, ravenous, and harpy laws.
Yet, shou'd I think, although the bill tak place,
The council winna lack sae meikle grace
As lat our heritage at wanworth gang,
Or the succeeding generations wrang
O' braw bein maintenance, and walth o' lear,
Whilk else had drappit to their children's skair;
For mony a deep, and mony a rare engine
Hae sprung frae Heriot's Wark, and sprung frae mine.

HERIOT

I find, my friend! that ye but little ken,
There's e'en now on the earth a set o' men,
Wha, if they get their private pouches lin'd,
Gie na a winnlestrae for a' mankind.
They'll sell their country, flae their conscience bare,
To gar the weigh-bauk turn a single hair.
The Government need only bait the line
Wi' the prevailin flee—the gowded coin!
Then our executors, and wise trustees,
Will sell them fishes in forbidden seas:
Upo' their dwinin country girn in sport;
Laugh in their sleeve, and get a place at court.

WATSON

Ere that day come, I'll 'mang our spirits pick
Some ghaist that trokes and conjures wi' Auld Nick,
To gar the wind wi' rougher rumbles blaw,
And weightier thuds than ever mortal saw:
Fireflaught and hail, wi' tenfauld fury's fires,
Shall lay yird-laigh Edina's airy spires:
Tweed shall rin rowtin down his banks out owre,
Till Scotland' out o' reach o' England's power;
Upo' the briny Borean jaws to float,
And mourn in dowie seughs her dowie lot.

HERIOT

Yonder's the tomb of wise Mackenzie fam'd,
Whase laws rebellious bigotry reclaim'd;
Freed the hale land o' covenantin fools,
Wha erst hae fash'd us wi' unnumberd'd dools.
Till night, we'll tak the swaird aboon our pows,
And then, whan she her ebon chariot rows,
We'll travel to the vau't wi' stealin stap,
And wauk Mackenzie frae his quiet nap;
Tell him our ails, that he, wi' wonted skill,
May fleg the schemers o' the Mortmain Bill.

GEORGE WATSON'S HOSPITAL

PLATE 28

*George Watson was an accountant to the Bank of Scotland and
died a bachelor in 1723, leaving £12,000 for the founding of a
school, which was started in 1738. The building has now been
incorporated into the new Royal Infirmary.*

FROM YARROW TO EDINBURGH COLLEGE

ALISON HAY DUNLOP

A SNOWSTORM set in towards the end of December. The shepherd meteorologists of the Borders recognised four kinds of snowflakes—Harefoot, Birdwing, Poppler, and Sparevvil. If the first snowstorm of the year was Harefoot, it betokened the storms of an old-fashioned winter. Harefoot flakes had fallen on Edinburgh College all night and all morning, and, though the sun had blinked out, it was evident that more snowflakes were coming.

I stood that day on the pavement, and was in the act of placing my class-books and Sir John Mandeville's *Lands* in the 'neuk' of my shepherd's maud, when I saw a stage-coach come in sight, driving heavily. It passed the College entrance, when, as if by concerted signal, while the guard blew a long, loud, defiant blast on his horn, the outside passengers delivered a volley of snowballs into the crowd of students who were thronging out of the gate. It was a short-sighted action, for snowball ammunition on the top of a stage-coach is necessarily limited. Another moment, and the street was darkened by the return charge,—snowballs from behind, and snowballs in front, snowballs to the right, and snowballs to the left. The guard's hat went far over the horses' heads, and the head-gear of the coachman and of the passengers followed in various pursuit; the glass windows were broken; a vociferous visage, purple of hue, was seen for one moment, to disappear the next,—and ball after ball went into the holes of the broken glass with a precision, a swiftness, and a glee, thrilling to the heart of a marksman.

The coachman held to his reins, and it was fortunate the horses had much of the spirit taken out of them with the heavy roads. In a wild way he tried to lash out with his whip: but it was no use. The enemy was everywhere in full pursuit, and the coach of the defiant blast, with its foolish freight, passed the Tron Church bruised, broken, battered, and beaten. Joyously we turned back to find that matters had wondrously developed in our absence, and, as we reached the College, the air seemed almost thick with snowballs.

A battle royal was raging, and this time against mettle—let me say it now—to the full as good as our own. It was the trades' dinner-hour; and we saw them—apprentices and young journeymen—pouring up from the Grassmarket and the Cowgate, gathering the snowballs and kneading them as they ran. Hitherto I had been fighting like David in Saul's armour; but to run with my plaid and Sir John Mandeville into Miss Swinton's—a mantua-maker on the South Bridge, who long rejoiced in a good south-country connection—was but the thought and the action of a moment, and then I was back in the thick of it, blood on fire, and every nerve tingling with a new, strange joy.

The battle consisted of charges and counter-charges as regards each main body. Once we were driven half-way up the quadrangle, and again we drove the enemy as far back as Hill Place, then in the course of erection—every man fighting with his whole heart and soul, and strength and hands. How could it be otherwise? Great Britain at that time was not only challenging all the history of modern nations, she was paling and dwarfing even the deeds of ancient Greece and Rome. Nelson was dead—his Edinburgh monument had been finished that year on the Calton Hill—but the glories of the Nile, and Copenhagen, and Trafalgar were a national inheritance. Wellington had but gone to the Peninsula, and already Vimiera and Talavera were the earnest of the British army's glory and its leader's future.

EDINBURGH UNIVERSITY AND SOUTH BRIDGE *c.*1820

PLATE 29

The building was designed by Robert Adam, the foundation stone being laid in 1789. The dome we see today was added at the end of the nineteenth century. The coach referred to in the fictional account opposite went away down South Bridge, at the bottom of which on the left is the spire of Tron Kirk.

LETTERS FROM EDINBURGH (1775)

EDWARD TOPHAM

THE PRESENT THEATRE is situated at the end of the New Bridge in the New Town, and on the outside is a plain structure like most others of the same nature. It was built by the subscription of a certain number of gentlemen, who let it originally to a manager for four hundred pounds a year. Mr Ross was the first person who took it, and his name was inserted in the patent, which made him manager as long as he chose. A few years ago, plays were not in that repute at Edinburgh they now are. The ministers, zealous for the good of their flock, preached against them, and the poor players were entirely routed: they have now, however, once more taken the field, and the clergy leave them to their ungodliness. During these contests, Mr Ross found, that the benefits of the theatre did not answer to the expences of it, and retreated in good time. Our modern Aristophanes, who imagined he had wit enough to laugh the Scotch out of their money, took it of Mr Ross at the same price that was originally paid for it. He brought on all his own comedies successively; but as most of the humour was local and particular, few people here understood it. Now and then, indeed, a very civil gentleman was so kind as to explain what he had been told in London, such a joke alluded to; but as jokes always lose their strength in travelling, nobody was the wiser for the explanation. But when, in the course of the acting, Mr Foote attempted to introduce the Minor upon the stage, the ministers, who had long lain dormant, now rose up in arms. The character of Mrs Cole gave them offence. They imagined themselves pointed out; but were so kind as to throw the injury upon religion. They acted just upon the same principles as the Monks did with Boccacio, who having told many ridiculous stories of their gluttony, and their amours in his Decameron, they very wisely agreed, that he had said many disrespectful things of religion in general. The Scotch Clergy, not contented with damning the play itself, very piously pronounced all those damned who went to see it. Parties, however, rose on this occasion; and many were so wicked as to insist on its being performed. Riots ensued: the unrighteous triumphed, and the poor play was performed.

THEATRE ROYAL

PLATE 30

*The theatre opened in 1769, when admission to the boxes and pit
was 3s, to the gallery 2s, and to the upper gallery 1s. Fifty years
later, when this engraving was published, box seats had gone up
to 5s, but the others were still the same price!*

REMINISCENCES

Thomas Carlyle

IN MY STUDENT DAYS the chosen Promenade of Edinburgh was Princes Street; from the East end of it, to and fro, westward as far as Frederick Street, or farther if you wished to be less jostled, and have the pavement more to yourself: there, on a bright afternoon, in its highest bloom probably about 4–5 P.M., all that was brightest in Edinburgh seemed to have stept out to enjoy, in the fresh pure air, the finest city-prospect in the world and the sight of one another, and was gaily streaming this way and that. From Castle Street or even the extreme west there was a visible increase in bright population, which thickened regularly eastward, and in the sections near the Register Office or extreme east, had become a fairly lively crowd, dense as it could find stepping-ground,—never needed to be denser, or to become a crush, so many side-streets offering you free issue all along, and the possibility of returning by a circuit, instead of abruptly on your steps. The crowd was lively enough, brilliant, many-coloured, many-voiced, clever-looking (beautiful and graceful young womankind a conspicuous element): crowd altogether elegant, polite, at its ease in the movements of it, as if or harmonious in the sound of its cheerful voices, bass and treble, fringed with the light laughters; a quite pretty kind of natural concert and rhythmus of march; into which, if at leisure, and carefully enough dressed (as some of us seldom were) you might introduce yourself, and flow for a turn or two with the general flood. It was finely convenient to a stranger in Edinburgh, intent to enjoy his eyes in instructive recreation; and see, or hope to see, so much of what was brightest and most distinguished in the place, on those easy terms. As for me, I never could afford to promenade or linger there; and only a few times, happened to float leisurely thro', on my way elsewhither. Which perhaps makes it look all the brighter now in far-off memory, being so *rare* as, in one sense, it surely is to me! Nothing of the same kind now remains in Edinburgh: already in 1832, you in vain sought and inquired Where the general promenade, then, was? The general promenade was, and continues, nowhere—as so many infinitely nobler things already do!

PRINCES STREET, EAST END, AND REGISTER OFFICE

PLATE 31

A view that has hardly changed. Opposite Register Office (see also plate 33) was the Theatre Royal (see also plate 30), on whose site now stands the General Post Office, the foundation stone of which was laid by the Prince Consort in 1861. The main post office at the time is farther up the street, in what is in effect the third block on the right.

LIFE OF PERCY BYSSHE SHELLEY

Thomas Jefferson Hogg

WE ENTERED Edinburgh in the dark, through mean, narrow streets, the aspect of which, by the faint light of dim lamps ill accorded with the magnificent promises of the splendour of the proud metropolis of the whole earth—of the capital of social elegance, and of perfect refinement.

I remained for the night at the wretched inn where the coach stopped, for I knew of no other, although it was a disgusting place. Nobody appeared to regard me. I didn't understand what they said; neither could I make the people understand me. In truth, they did not care to know what I wanted. However, I succeeded, with some difficulty, in catching hold of a stupid, red-haired, bare-necked, barefooted, dirty girl, by the arm; I held her fast, and made her conduct me upstairs to a squalid little bedroom. When we got there, she found out what I required: another light, besides that which she held in her hand, broke upon her, and she exclaimed with vivacity: 'Oh! you will want a chamber'. I observed the impressions of naked and muddy feet, of bare toes and heels, on the hearth and on the floor, but no other traces of social elegance: the young wench was half naked, as it was; had she been stark, most assuredly I should not have taken her for one of the three Graces, whatever the little lecturer might have affirmed. I took the candle from her, and she withdrew, muttering some words of her sweet northern Doric, which probably signified, 'Good night!' The bed was less distasteful than the chamber. I had passed thirty hours or more in the open air on the top of the coach, and had travelled two hundred miles: this was a powerful opiate.

If such be, in very deed, the beauteous city of Minerva, the chosen residence of Apollo and the Muses, the true abode of Beauty, of the Loves and Graces, I wish I were back again at my lodgings in York, or at one of the inns near the lakes, which tourists report as comfortable! But a sound refreshing sleep soon put an end to all reflections, wishes, and regrets: I made one sleep.

When I awoke in the morning, it was quite light: bell there was none; calling out, however loud, was disregarded, my little sylph would not come, nor would any of her fairy sisters, if she had any. I put on my clothes, and went downstairs into a common room, an uncommonly dirty, dingy hole; here I procured some breakfast, which was not so much amiss. I then sallied forth to discover if the rest of the New Jerusalem was as mean and shabby as what I had already seen; I more than half suspected that it was. I soon emerged from the narrow streets; and then, O! glorious spectacle, by force of contrast made still more noble, more glorious; I wandered about, lost in admiration. I ascended the Castle Hill, the Calton Hill, my delight still increasing. Yet it

EDINBURGH CASTLE FROM THE GRASSMARKET

PLATE 32

The building on the left is the old Corn Exchange.

was a meeting of extremes: I beheld magnificence—triumphs of art and nature; yet I saw many odious and revolting objects, which I had never met with, even in the poorest places in England, and which I forbear to describe.

Having at once satisfied and inflamed my curiosity, I began to think of the main purpose of my long journey—my college friend. I had written to him that I would join him here, but I had not given him any address, for I did not know any, neither had I received a direction from him. Was there a better, a speedier course, than the hope of a chance meeting in the streets of a large city? I bethought me of the post office; he might have sent a letter for me thither. I was standing musing on the bridge which connects the new town with the old: a grave, white, middle-aged man was passing. I inquired of him for the post office.

'Come with me, I am going there myself. You are a stranger?'

'Yes.'

'You never saw so fine a bridge as this is, I am very sure. It is the finest in the known world!'

'I have seen a finer river, one with more water in it.'

He seemed much disconcerted. I told him how I was situated.

'They will give you the address you require at the post office, they are sure to have it; we will go to the post office together; but you must first see our new university, as you are a stranger.'

We passed the post office and came to a large building, not only unfinished, but not in progress. It appeared that the work had ceased for want of funds.[1]

'What do you think of that, sir?'

'When it is completed it will be a very handsome building, and, I dare say, very commodious.'

'Not only that, but if all the buildings at Oxford and Cambridge were moulded and amalgamated together into one edifice, the effect would not be the same; it would be far inferior!'

I had learned that it was most discreet to be silent. We returned to the post office. There was no letter for me, but they gave me my friend's address in George Street. Whether he had left it there for me, or for his own letters, I did not ask.

'I am going in that direction myself. I will point out George Street to you.'

We returned on our steps.

'That is the Register Office,' said my kind, grave guide; 'it is the finest building on the habitable earth.'

I looked him in the face; I had wounded his feelings about the bridge, without it at all diminishing his obliging good nature, so I held my peace.

[1] The main post office was then (in 1811) at the end of a row of buildings which stood on the western side of the bridge (see plate 43). The University (see plate 29) took 45 years to build, and even then was still without its dome.

REGISTER OFFICE 1820

PLATE 33

Started in 1774 to a plan by Robert Adam, but not finally
completed until 1834.

'It is universally acknowledged to be so! But you must see the interior!'

We entered it; it was a handsome structure, certainly; perhaps needlessly large. We walked along Princes Street together, at the corner of a cross street he took leave of me with sundry profound solemn bows, having previously pointed out George Street. I soon set foot in George Street, a spacious, noble, well-built street; but a deserted street, or rather a street which people had not yet come fully to inhabit. I soon found the number indicated at the post office; I have forgotten it, but it was on the left side— the side next to Princes Street. I knocked at the door of a handsome house; it was all right; and in a handsome front parlour I was presently received rapturously by my friend.[1] He looked just as he used to look at Oxford, and as he looked when I saw him in last April, in our trellised apartment; but now joyous at meeting again, not as then sad at parting. I also saw—and for the first time— his lovely young bride, bright as the morning—as the morning of that bright day on which we first met; bright, blooming, radiant with youth, health, and beauty. I was hailed triumphantly by the new-married pair; my arrival was more than welcome; they had got my letter and expected to rejoice at my coming every moment. 'We have met at last once more!' Shelley exclaimed, 'and we will never part again! You must have a bed in the house!' It was deemed necessary, indispensable. At that time of life a bed a mile or two off, as far as I was concerned, would have done as well; but I must have a bed in the house. The landlord was summoned, he came instantly; a bed in the house; the necessity was so urgent that they did not give him time to speak. When the poor man was permitted to answer, he said, 'I have a spare bedroom, but it is at the top of the house. It may not be quite so pleasant.' He conducted my up a handsome stone staircase of easiest ascent; the way was not difficult, but very long. It appeared well nigh interminable. We came at length to an airy, spacious bedroom. 'This will do very well.' A stone staircase is handsome and commodious, and, in case of fire, it must be a valuable security; but whenever a door was shut it thundered; the thunder rolled pealing for some seconds. I was to lodge with Jupiter Tonans at the top of Olympus. Of all the houses in London, with which I am acquainted, those in Fitzroy Square alone remind me, by their sonorous powers, of Edinburgh, and of the happy days which I passed in that beautiful city. On returning to my friends our mutual greetings were repeated; each had a thousand things to tell and to ask of the rest. Our joy being a little calmed, we agreed to walk. 'We are in the capital of the unfortunate

[1] See page 109.

76

GEORGE STREET AND ST ANDREW'S CHURCH

PLATE 34

*The church was designed by a George Street resident, Major
Andrew Fraser, in 1785. The spire was added in 1789.*

Queen Mary,' said Harriet; 'we must see her palace first of all.' We soon found Holyrood House; a beggarly palace, in truth. We saw the long line of Scottish monarchs, from Fergus the First downwards, disposed in two rows, being evidently the productions of some very inferior artist, who could not get employment as a sign-painter. We saw Mary's bedroom, the stains of Rizzio's blood, and all the other relics. These objects, intrinsically mean and paltry, greatly interested my companions, especially Harriet, who was well-read in the sorrowful history of the unhappy queen. Bysshe must go home and write letters, I was to ascend Arthur's Seat with the lady. We marched up the steep hill boldly, and reached the summit. The view may be easily seen, it is impossible to describe it. It was a thousand pities Bysshe was not with us, and then we might remain there; one ought never to quit so lovely a scene.

'Let us sit down; probably when he has finished writing he will come to us.'

We sat a long time, at first gazing around, afterwards we looked out for the young bridegroom, but he did not appear. It was fine while we ascended; it was fine, sunny, clear, and still, whilst we remained on the top; but when we began to descend, the wind commenced blowing. Harriet refused to proceed; she sat down again on the rock, and declared that we would remain there for ever! For ever is rather a long time; to sit until the wind abated would have been to sit there quite long enough. Entreaties were in vain. I was hungry, for I had not dined on either of the two preceding days. The sentence—never to dine again—was a severe one, and although it was pronounced by the lips of beauty, I ventured to appeal against it; so I left her and proceeded slowly down the hill, the wind blowing fresh. She sat for some time longer, but finding that I was in earnest, she came running down after me. Harriet was always most unwilling to show her ankles, or even her feet, hence her reluctance to move in the presence of a rude, indelicate wind, which did not respect her modest scrupulousness. If there was not much to admire about these carefully-concealed ankles, certainly there was nothing to blame.

HOLYROOD PALACE, PART OF THE WEST FRONT

PLATE 35

*Queen Mary's apartments occupied the second floor of the turret:
the Picture Gallery is behind the turret, on the north side of the
Palace.*

A MIDNIGHT VISIT TO HOLYROOD

COUNTESS OF CAITHNESS

I DESIRED nothing better than to meet dear Marie alone, and also thought she would thus be more likely to come to me than if I went accompanied by another. And so I gathered my dress around me, and stepped reverently and solemnly over the graves of my husband's family, which occupy the centre of what was once the nave, preferring this open space to the deeper shadows of the side aisles, which looked weird and awful in the darkness.

It was an intensely dark night, and the brightness and brilliancy of the stars above only served to make the earthly darkness more visible.

Never, never, I thought, could this once lovely chapel have looked more beautiful than it did at this moment; instead of the pealing notes of the organ, sackbut, harp, lute, and dulcimer, and all the lovely instruments that once resounded through its many arches, it was now pervaded by a still more solemn silence; instead of lighted torches and the innumerable wax tapers that once blazed upon its altars, it was now lighted alone by the stars of heaven, and these looked in upon me from all sides through each gothic window, and from the deep blue of the canopy that was my only roof, and their vast dwelling-place.

Thus thinking, I reached the glorious eastern window where the high altar once stood, but which now looks down upon the green grass and a few broken stones. On one of these I knelt, and lifting up my eyes and my thoughts to heaven, prayed long and fervently for my sweet guardian, who had once, as she said, knelt on this very spot, decked in all the bravery of a bride, to plight her troth to the handsome Darnley. His *grave* now stood under the cloister close at my right hand, and that of the man he had made so celebrated, poor, murdered David Rizzio, I had passed near the entrance door.

'Where are they all now?' I exclaimed aloud, and 'where are you, my own dear, ever beautiful, my precious Marie?'

'Here, with you,' exclaimed a soft low voice at my side, and, as I turned, I beheld a faint and shadowy form, more like a cloud or a grey mist than a living being, but which gradually assumed a whiter and more tangible appearance.

'You see I have kept my word,' she continued, and from that moment she commenced, and poured forth one of the most sublime and glorious addresses I have ever heard. Indeed, I have never heard or read anything like it. Vainly did I afterwards try to record what she had said, though the spirit of it will ever live in my memory, and must ever bear its influence on my future life; yet, the words in which it was uttered I found afterwards had quite escaped my powers of retention.

Suffice it to say, that no allusion to the past, not one word of the time when she had last stood on that sacred spot, the Sovereign of the land, sullied the calm midnight air, or the purity of the overshadowing heavens—not one word but what angels would love to listen to, and what they, doubtless, did listen to with advantage, fell upon my deeply reverent and attentive ear.

The Marie who spoke was the Marie of the Star Circle, of which she had before declared to me she was one of the messengers—a circle of pure, great, and holy ones, whose most earnest endeavour is to unite man to God—to bring heaven nearer to earth, by leading those who are ready for it out of the terrible mire of social evils, and inaugurating the era of universal righteousness prophesied of old.

HOLYROOD CHAPEL

PLATE 36

Looking down towards the west door.

MARRIAGE

S USAN F ERRIER

ALL MARY'S sensations of admiration were faint compared to those she experienced as she viewed the Scottish metropolis. It was associated in her mind with all the local prepossessions to which youth and enthusiasm love to give 'a local habitation and a name'; and visions of older times floated o'er her mind as she gazed on its rocky battlements, and traversed the lonely arcades of its deserted palace.

'And this was once a gay court!' thought she, as she listened to the dreary echo of her own footsteps; 'and this very ground on which I now stand was trod by the hapless Mary Stuart! Her eye beheld the same objects that mine now rests upon; her hand has touched the draperies I now hold in mine. These frail memorials remain; but what remains of Scotland's Queen but a blighted name!'

Even the bloodstained chamber possessed a nameless charm for Mary's vivid imagination. She had not entirely escaped the superstitions of the country in which she had lived; and she readily yielded her assent to the asseverations of her guide and to its being the *bona fide* blood of *David Rizzio*, which for nearly three hundred years had resisted all human efforts to efface.

'My credulity is so harmless,' said she in answer to her uncle's attempt to laugh her out of her belief, 'that I surely may be permitted to indulge it—especially since I confess I feel a sort of indescribable pleasure in it.'

'You take a pleasure in the sight of blood!' exclaimed Mr Douglas in astonishment, 'you who turn pale at sight of a cut finger, and shudder at a leg of mutton with the juice in it!'

'Oh! mere modern vulgar blood is very shocking,' answered Mary, with a smile; 'but observe how this is mellowed by time into a tint that could not offend the most fastidious fine lady; besides,' added she in a graver tone, 'I own I love to believe in things supernatural; it seems to connect us more with another world than when everything is seen to proceed in the mere ordinary course of nature, as it is called. I cannot bear to imagine a dreary chasm betwixt the inhabitants of this world and beings of a higher sphere; I love to fancy myself surrounded by—

'I wish to heaven you would remember you are surrounded by rational beings, and not fall into such rhapsodies,' said her uncle, glancing at a party who stood near them, jesting upon all the objects which Mary had been regarding with so much veneration. 'But come, you have been long enough here. Let us try whether a breeze on the Calton Hill will not dispel these cobwebs from your brain.'

The day, though cold, was clear and sunny; and the lovely spectacle before them shone forth in all its gay magnificence. The blue waters lay calm and motionless. The opposite shores glowed in a thousand varied tints of wood and plain, rock and mountain, cultured field and purple moor. Beneath, the old town reared its dark brow, and the new one stretched its golden lines; while all around the varied charms of nature lay scattered in that profusion which nature's hand alone can bestow.

'Oh! this is exquisite!' exclaimed Mary after a long pause, in which she had been riveted in admiration of the scene before her. 'And you are in the right, my dear uncle. The ideas which are inspired by the contemplation of such a spectacle as this are far—oh, how far!—superior to those excited by the mere works of art. There I can, at best, think but of the inferior agents of Providence; here the soul rises from nature up to nature's God.'

'Upon my soul, you will be taken for a Methodist, Mary, if you talk in this manner,' said Mr Douglas, with some marks of disquiet, as he turned round at the salutation of a fat elderly gentleman, whom he presently recognised as Bailie Broadfoot.

The first salutations over, Mr Douglas's fears of Mary having been overheard recurred, and he felt anxious to

HOLYROOD PALACE—THE INNER COURT

PLATE 37

This engraving was published in 1819, just a year after the appearance of Susan Ferrier's novel.

remove any unfavourable impression with regard to his own principles, at least, from the mind of the enlightened magistrate.

'Your fine views here have set my niece absolutely raving,' said he, with a smile; 'but I tell her it is only in romantic minds that fine scenery inspires romantic ideas. I daresay many of the worthy inhabitants of Edinburgh walk here with no other idea than that of sharpening their appetites for dinner.'

'Nae doot,' said the Bailie, 'it's a most capital place for that. Were it no' for that I ken nae muckle use it would be of.'

'You speak from experience of its virtues in that respect, I suppose?' said Mr Douglas gravely.

''Deed, as to that I canna compleen. At times, to be sure, I am troubled with a little kind of squeamishness after our public interteenments; but three rounds o' the hill sets a' to rights.'

Then observing Mary's eyes exploring, as he supposed, the town of Leith, 'You see that prospeck to nae advantage the day, miss,' said he. 'If the glass-houses had been workin', it would have looked as weel again. Ye hae nae glass-houses in the Highlands; na, na.'

The Bailie had a share in the concern; and the volcanic clouds of smoke that issued from thence were far more interesting subjects of speculation to him than all the eruptions of Vesuvius or Etna. But there was nothing to charm the lingering view to-day; and he therefore proposed their taking a look at Bridewell, which, next to the smoke from the glass-houses, he reckoned the object most worthy of notice. It was indeed deserving of the praises bestowed upon it; and Mary was giving her whole attention to the details of it when she was suddenly startled by hearing her own name wailed in piteous accents from one of the lower cells, and, upon turning round, she discovered in the prisoner the son of one of the tenants of Glenfern. Duncan M'Free had always been looked upon as a very honest lad in the Highlands, but he had left home to push his fortune as a pedlar; and the temptations of the low country having proved too much for his virtue, poor Duncan was now expiating his offence in durance vile.

'I shall have a pretty account of you to carry to Glenfern,' said Mr Douglas, regarding the culprit with his sternest look.

'Oh 'deed, sir, it's no' my faut!' answered Duncan, blubbering bitterly; 'but there's nae freedom at a' in this country. Lord, an' I war oot o't! Ane canna ca' their head their ain in't; for ye canna lift the bouk o' a prin but they're a' upon ye.' And a fresh burst of sorrow ensued.

Finding the *peccadillo* was of a venial nature, Mr Douglas besought the Bailie to use his interest to procure the enfranchisement of this his vassal, which Mr Broadfoot, happy to oblige a good customer, promised should be obtained on the following day; and Duncan's emotions being rather clamorous, the party found it necessary to withdraw.

'And noo,' said the Bailie, as they emerged from this place of dole and durance, 'will ye step up to the monument, and tak a rest and some refreshment?'

'Rest and refreshment in a monument!' exclaimed Mr Douglas. 'Excuse me, my good friend, but we are not inclined to bait there yet a while.'

The Bailie did not comprehend the joke; and he proceeded in his own drawling humdrum accent to assure them that the monument was a most convenient place.

'It was erected in honour of Lord Neilson's memory,' said he, 'and is let aff to a pastrycook and confectioner, where you can always find some trifles to treat the ladies, such as pies and custards, and berries, and these sort of things; but we passed an order in the cooncil that there should be naething of a spirituous nature introduced; for if ance spirits got admittance there's no saying what might happen.'

This was a fact which none of the party were disposed to dispute; and the Bailie, triumphing in his dominion over the spirits, shuffled on before to do the honours of this place, appropriated at one and the same time to the manes of a hero and the making of minced pies. The regale was admirable, and Mary could not help thinking times were improved, and that it was a better thing to eat tarts in Lord Nelson's Monument than to have been poisoned in Julius Caesar's.

CALTON HILL 1818

PLATE 38

Bridewell, the 'house of correction', is the circular building immediately below Nelson's Monument. To the west of it are the castellated towers of the Governor's House of the New Jail, *finished in 1816. In the foreground is Trinity College Chapel, shortly afterwards to be pulled down to make way for railway sidings.*

PICTURESQUE NOTES ON EDINBURGH

ROBERT LOUIS STEVENSON

OF ALL PLACES for a view, this Calton Hill is perhaps the best; since you can see the Castle, which you lose from the Castle, and Arthur's Seat, which you cannot see from Arthur's Seat. It is the place to stroll on one of those days of sunshine and east wind which are so common in our more than temperate summer. The breeze comes off the sea, with a little of freshness, and that touch of chill, peculiar to the quarter, which is delightful to certain very ruddy organisations and greatly the reverse to the majority of mankind. It brings with it a faint, floating haze, a cunning decolouriser, although not thick enough to obscure outlines near at hand. But the haze lies more thickly to windward at the far end of Musselburgh Bay; and over the Links of Aberlady and Berwick Law and the hump of the Bass Rock it assumes the aspect of a bank of thin sea fog.

Immediately underneath upon the south, you command the yards of the High School, and the towers of the new Jail—a large place, castellated to the extent of folly, standing by itself on the edge of a steep cliff, and often joyfully hailed by tourists as the Castle. In the one, you may perhaps see female prisoners taking exercise like a string of nuns; in the other, schoolboys running at play and their shadows keeping step with them. From the bottom of the valley, a gigantic chimney rises almost to the level of the eye, a taller and a shapelier edifice than Nelson's Monument. Look a little farther, and there is Holyrood Palace, with its Gothic front and ruined abbey, and the red sentry pacing smartly to and fro before the door like a mechanical figure in a panorama. By way of an outpost, you can single out the little peak-roofed lodge, over which Rizzio's murderers made their escape and where Queen Mary herself, according to gossip, bathed in white wine to entertain her loveliness. Behind and overhead, lie the Queen's Park, from Muschat's Cairn to Dumbiedykes, St Margaret's Loch, and the long wall of Salisbury Crags; and thence, by knoll and rocky bulwark and precipitous slope, the eye rises to the top of Arthur's Seat, a hill for magnitude, a mountain in virtue of its bold design.

Queen Mary's Bath House. This sixteenth-century building is reputed to be the route by which the murderers of Rizzio escaped and where Mary herself used to bathe in wine—certainly there was at one time a spring of fine water underneath it.

HOLYROOD PALACE FROM CALTON HILL

PLATE 39

This view, drawn some 25 years before Stevenson's birth, nevertheless illustrates much of what excited him about it. The 'shapelier edifice than Nelson's Column' was in fact the chimney of the gasworks (see plate 40). Queen Mary's Bath House would be on the line between the left-hand seated figure and the north side of Holyrood Chapel.

LIFE JOTTINGS OF AN OLD EDINBURGH CITIZEN

Sir J H A Macdonald (Lord Kingsburgh)

DURING BOYHOOD, one naturally saw more of our native city than when all the walks were 'on the chain,' in the control of nurses and governesses. Many a visit did I pay with my companions to the Calton Hill, where there was the best place near home for kite-flying. At the time the hill, which is a valuable asset as a place of beauty and recreation, presented some features which one can only recall with shame. The upper part of it was frequently occupied as a place for beating carpets with flails, which sent clouds of insanitary dust over the neighbouring ground, and into the mouths and nostrils of the children who came to the hill to play there. On the north slope linen was washed, and the ground slopped around water-cocks which should never have been allowed to disfigure the scene. The washings were hung up on ropes stretched on shabby, badly set-up poles, disfiguring the view in a manner altogether shameful. The space at the back of the great pillars, which tell of Scotland's folly in attempting to build a great national monument, was enclosed by a high paling fence resembling a builder's yard, large placards informing the public that for sixpence a head they could see 'Forrest's Statuary' within. We boys wondered what our deficiency in sixpences was depriving us of, but having since seen some of the so-called statuary, it is not possible to do otherwise than wonder that our municipal fathers should have condescended to let the city's property in order to enable Mr Forrest to draw money by showing his so-called artistic productions. The enclosure was hideous and discreditable, and the contents were unworthy to be provided with accommodation on our classical hill. It was only by an effort of the citizens that the Town Council were prevented from placing these inartistic figures as adornments (!) to the main walk of West Princes Street Gardens! Farther eastwards one Miss Short had succeeded, after several efforts, in leasing a space for what was called an Observatory, a mean wooden erection, where a *camera lucida* or *obscura*—I forget which—enabled the visitor to see the country round on a flat, white table, and where at night an inferior telescope gave a view of the heavens.

NELSON'S MONUMENT AND THE NATIONAL MONUMENT
ON CALTON HILL 1845

PLATE 40

Nelson's Monument was completed in 1816. The National Monument was started in 1822 but never completed—the money ran out after twelve columns had been erected. This view was drawn when Macdonald was about eight years old and may *safely be taken to illustrate his recollections. Even the fence is there! Also the gasworks' chimney to which Stevenson refers (page 86).*

MEMORIALS OF HIS TIME

LORD COCKBURN

THE YEAR 1808 saw the commencement of our new jail on the Calton Hill. It was a piece of undoubted bad taste to give so glorious an eminence to a prison. It was one of our noblest sites, and would have been given by Pericles to one of his finest edifices. But in modern towns, though we may abuse and bemoan, we must take what we can get. Princes Street was then closed at its east end by a line of mean houses running north and south. All to the east of these houses was a burial ground, of which the southern portion still remains; and the way of reaching the Calton Hill was to go, by Leith Street, to its base (as may still be done), and then up the steep, narrow, stinking, spiral street which still remains, and was then the only approach. Scarcely any sacrifice could be too great that removed the houses from the end of Princes Street, and made a level road to the hill, or, in other words, produced Waterloo Bridge. The effect was like the drawing up of the curtain in the theatre. But the bridge would never have been where it is except for the jail. The lieges were taxed for the prison; and luckily few of them were aware that they were also taxed for the bridge as the prison's access. In all this magnificent improvement, which in truth gave us the hill and all its decoration, there was scarcely one particle of prospective taste. The houses alongside the bridge were made handsome by the specula-tors for their own interest; but the general effect of the new level opening into Princes Street, and its consequences, were planned or foreseen by nobody.

The completion of the new jail implied the removal of the old one: and accordingly in a few years after this 'The Heart of Midlothian' ceased to beat. A most atrocious jail it was, the very breath of which almost struck down any stranger who entered its dismal door; and as ill placed as possible, without one inch of ground beyond its black and horrid walls. And these walls were very small: the entire hole being filled with little dark cells; heavy manacles the only security; airless, waterless, drainless; a living grave. One week of that dirty, fetid, cruel torture-house was a severer punishment than a year of our worst modern prison—more dreadful in its sufferings, more certain its corruption, overwhelming the innocent with a more tremendous sense of despair, provoking the guilty to more audacious defiance. But yet I wish the building had been spared. It was of great age: it once held the Parliament (though *how* it could, I can't conceive): it was incorporated with much curious history; and its outside was picturesque. Neither exposing St Giles, nor widening the street, nor any other such object, ought to have been allowed to extinguish so interesting a relic.

NEW JAIL AND PRINCES STREET FROM CALTON HILL

PLATE 41

*The opposite view to plate 31. The New Jail was demolished in
1938 to make way for St Andrew's House, though the
Governor's House survives. 'The Heart of Midlothian' was the
Tolbooth (see plate 21).*

THE MISADVENTURES
OF
JOHN NICHOLSON

R OBERT L OUIS S TEVENSON

CLOSE UNDER the Calton Hill there runs a certain narrow avenue, part street, part by-road. The head of it faces the doors of the prison; its tail descends into the sunless slums of the Low Calton. One one hand it is overhung by the crags of the hill, on the other by an old grave-yard. Between these two the road-way runs in a trench, sparsely lighted at night, sparsely frequented by day, and bordered, when it has cleared the place of tombs, by dingy and ambiguous houses. One of these was the house of Collette; and at this door our ill-starred John was presently beating for admittance. In an evil hour he satisfied the jealous inquiries of the contraband hotelkeeper; in an evil hour he penetrated into the somewhat unsavoury interior. Alan, to be sure, was there, seated in a room lighted by noisy gas-jets, beside a dirty table-cloth, engaged on a coarse meal, and in the company of several tipsy members of the junior bar. But Alan was not sober; he had lost a thousand pounds upon a horse-race, had received the news at dinner-time, and was now, in default of any possible means of extrication, drowning the memory of his predicament. He to help John! The thing was impossible; he couldn't help himself.

'If you have a beast of a father,' said he, 'I can tell you I have a brute of a trustee.'

LOWER PART OF CALTON HILL, WITH THE PRISON BEHIND

PLATE 42

LETTERS FROM EDINBURGH

EDWARD TOPHAM

THE MOST particular effect which I find of this Climate, is the Winds; which here reign in all their violence, and seem indeed to claim the country as their own. A person, who has passed all his time in England, cannot be said to know what a wind is: he has zephyrs, and breezes, and gales, but nothing more; at least they appear so to me after having felt the hurricanes of Scotland.

As this Town is situated on the borders of the sea, and surrounded by hills of an immense height, the currents of air are carried down between them with a rapidity and a violence which nothing can resist. It has frequently been known, that in the New Town at Edinburgh three or four people have scarce been able to shut the door of the house; and it is a very common accident to hear of sedan chairs being overturned. It seems almost a necessary compliment here, to wait upon a lady the next morning, to hope she got safe home. . . .

At other times, the winds, instead of rushing down with impetuosity, whirl about in eddies, and become still more dreadful. On these occasions it is almost impossible to stir out of doors, as the dust and stones gathered up in these vortices not only prevent your seeing, but frequently cut your legs by the velocity with which they are driven. The Scotch have a particular appellation for this, *'The Stour'*.

The chief scene where the winds exert their influence, is the New Bridge, which, by being thrown over a long valley that is open at both ends, and particularly from being ballustraded on each side, admits the wind in the most charming manner imaginable; and you receive it with the same force you would do, were it conveyed to you through a pair of bellows. It is far from unentertaining for a man to pass over this bridge on a tempestuous day. In walking over it this morning I had the pleasure of adjusting a lady's petticoats which had blown almost entirely over her head, and which prevented her disengaging herself from the situation she was in: but in charity to her distresses, I concealed her charms from public view: one poor gentleman, who was rather too much engaged with the novelty of the objects before him, unfortunately forgot his own hat and wig, which were lifted up by an unpremeditated puff, and carried entirely away.

But though the bleak air of this Climate may give, as it is said to do, that keen penetrating look to the inhabitants, which they certainly posses, as well as great activity of body, they are far from being healthy in general. I have scarce met with one instance of remarkable longevity amongst all the people I have seen, and there are very few places where you observe more funerals. Whether this is to be attributed entirely to the climate, or in some part to the College of Physicians, who are very eminent in their profession, I leave you to determine for yourself.

There is one circumstance here which certainly deserves notice, as it is a contradiction to all the rules which are laid down in regard to climates; I mean, the early maturity of their women. It is generally imagined that cold has the same degree of influence over the animal, as it has over the vegetable world; but in this country they are in direct opposition; for the plants are very late, and the girls extremely forward.

THE NEW, OR NORTH, BRIDGE FROM THE SOUTH 1818

PLATE 43

The foundation stone was laid in 1763 before there was any detailed architect's plan. The bridge was opened to pedestrians in 1769 but later that same year part of it fell down, burying five people. It was finally completed in 1772, and rebuilt 1896-97.

The erection of the buildings on its west side, the nearest of which at one time housed the post office (see page 74) caused such controversy that a meeting was held in 1817 to halt further progress.

LONDON JOURNAL

WE TALKED of Scotland. Ogilvie, who is a rank Scot, defended his native land with all the powers that he could muster up. I was diverted to see how great a man a London wit is in comparison of one of your country swans who sing ever so *bonnily*. Ogilvie said there was a very rich country round Edinburgh. 'No, no,' said Goldsmith, with a sneering laugh: 'it is not a rich country.' Ogilvie then said that Scotland has a great many noble wild prospects. 'Sir,' said Johnson, 'I believe you have a great many noble wild prospects; and Lapland is remarkable for prodigious noble wild prospects. But, Sir, I believe the noblest prospect that a Scotsman ever sees is the road which leads him to England!'

We gave a roar of applause to this most excellent sally of strong humour. At the same time, I could not help thinking that Dr Johnson showed want of taste in laughing at the wild grandeur of nature, which to a mind undebauched by art conveys the most pleasing awful sublime ideas. Have I not experienced the full force of this when gazing at thee, O Arthur Seat, thou venerable mountain! whether in the severity of winter thy brow has been covered with snow or wrapped in mist; or in the gentle mildness of summer the evening sun has shone upon thy verdant sides diversified with rugged moss-clad rocks and rendered religious by the ancient chapel of St Anthony. Beloved hill, the admiration of my youth! Thy noble image shall ever fill my mind! Let me travel over the whole earth, I shall still remember thee; and when I return to my native country, while I live I will visit thee with affection and reverence!

ARTHUR'S SEAT AND HOLYROOD PALACE

PLATE 44

THE HEART OF MIDLOTHIAN

SIR WALTER SCOTT

ARTHUR'S SEAT shall be my bed,
  The sheets shall ne'er be pressed by me;
St Anton's well shall be my drink,
  Sin' my true-love's forsaken me.

Old Song

If I were to chose a spot from which the rising or setting sun could be seen to greatest possible advantage, it would be that wild path winding around the foot of the high belt of semicircular rocks, called Salisbury Crags, and marking the verge of the steep descent which slopes down into the glen on the south-eastern side of the city of Edinburgh. The prospect, in its general outline, commands a close-built, high-piled city, stretching itself out beneath in a form, which, to romantic imagination, may be supposed to represent that of a dragon; now, a noble arm of the sea, with its rocks, isles, distant shores, and boundary of mountains; and now, a fair and fertile champaign country, varied with hill, dale, and rock, and skirted by the picturesque ridge of the Pentland mountains. But as the path gently circles around the base of the cliffs, the prospect, composed as it is of these enchanting and sublime objects, changes at every step, and presents them blended with, or divided from, each other, in every possible variety which can gratify the eye and the imagination. When a piece of scenery so beautiful, yet so varied,—so exciting by its intricacy, and yet so sublime,—is lighted up by the tints of morning or of evening, and displays all that variety of shadowy depth, exchanged with partial brilliancy, which gives character even to the tamest of landscapes, the effect approaches near to enchantment. This path used to be my favourite evening and morning resort, when engaged with a favourite author, or new subject of study.

EDINBURGH FROM THE FOOT OF SALISBURY CRAGS

PLATE 45

The passage follows closely that quoted on pp. 50-56, and this view was drawn only about six years after the publication of Scott's novel in 1818. The buildings on the far sky-line are, from left to right: Heriot's Hospital, Castle, St Giles', Tron Church,

St George's Church in Charlotte Square (1811), St Andrew's Church, Melville Monument (1821), New Jail, Bridewell. The tower in the left foreground below the Castle belongs to the old Royal Infirmary.

RECOLLECTIONS OF A TOUR MADE IN SCOTLAND IN 1803

Dorothy Wordsworth

ARRIVED AT Edinburgh a little before sunset. As we approached, the Castle rock resembling that of Stirling—in the same manner appearing to rise from a plain of cultivated ground, the Firth of Forth being on the other side, and not visible. Drove to the White Hart in the Grassmarket, an inn which had been mentioned to us, and which we conjectured would better suit us than one in a more fashionable part of the town. It was not noisy, and tolerably cheap. Drank tea, and walked up to the Castle, which luckily was very near. Much of the daylight was gone; so that except it had been a clear evening, which it was not, we could not have seen the distant prospect.

September 16th, Friday. The sky the evening before, as you may remember the ostler told us, had been *gay and dull*, and this morning it was downright dismal: very dark, and promising nothing but a wet day, and before breakfast was over the rain began, though not heavily. We set out upon our walk, and went through many streets to Holyrood House, and thence to the hill called Arthur's Seat, a high hill, very rocky at the top, and below covered with smooth turf, on which sheep were feeding. We climbed up till we came to St Anthony's Well and *Chapel*, as it is called, but it is more like a hermitage than a chapel,—a small ruin, which from its situation is exceedingly interesting, though in itself not remarkable. We sate down on a stone not far from the chapel, over-looking a pastoral hollow as wild and solitary as any in the heart of the Highland mountains: there, instead of the roaring of torrents, we listened to the noises of the city which were blended in one loud indistinct buzz, a regular sound in the air, which in certain moods of feeling, and at certain times, might have a more tranquillizing effect upon the mind than in those which we are accustomed to hear in such places. The Castle rock looked exceedingly large through the misty air: a cloud of black smoke over-hung the city, which combined with the rain and mist to conceal the shapes of the houses, an obscurity which added much to the grandeur of the sound that proceeded from it. It was impossible to think of anything that was little or mean, the goings-on of trade, the strife of men, or every-day city business; the impression was one, and it was visionary, like the conceptions of our childhood of Bagdad or Balsora when we have been reading the Arabian Nights' Entertainments. Though the rain was very heavy we remained upon the hill for some time, then returned by the same road by which we had come, through the green flat fields, formerly the pleasure-grounds of Holyrood House, on the edge of which stands the old roofless chapel of venerable architecture. It is a pity that it should be suffered to fall down, for the walls appear to be yet entire. Very near to the chapel is Holyrood House, which we could not but lament has nothing ancient in its appearance, being sash-windowed and not an irregular pile. It is very like a building for some national establishment, a hospital for soldiers or sailors.

ST ANTHONY'S CHAPEL ON ARTHUR'S SEAT

PLATE 46

*The fifteenth-century ruin is of obscure origin, but the chapel was
probably built by the Knights Templar of St Anthony at Leith.*

LIFE OF SIR WALTER SCOTT

John Gibson Lockhart

REGALIA OF SCOTLAND

THE TIME now approached when a Commission to examine the Crown-room in the Castle of Edinburgh, which had sprung from one of Scott's conversations with the Prince Regent in 1815, was at length to be acted upon; and the result was the discovery of the long lost regalia of Scotland. Of the official proceedings of the 4th Feb. 1818, the reader has a full and particular account in an Essay which Scott penned shortly afterwards; but I may add a little incident of the 5th. He and several of his brother Commissioners then revisited the Castle, accompanied by some of the ladies of their families. His daughter Sophia told me that her father's conversation had worked her feelings up to such a pitch, that when the lid was again removed, she nearly fainted, and drew back from the circle. As she was retiring, she was startled by his voice exclaiming, in a tone of the deepest emotion, 'something between anger and despair,' as she expressed it, 'By G—, No!' One of the Commissioners, not quite entering into the solemnity with which Scott regarded this business, had it seems made a sort of motion as if he meant to put the crown on the head of one of the young ladies near him, but the voice and aspect of the Poet were more than sufficient to make the worthy gentleman understand his error; and respecting the enthusiasm with which he had not been taught to sympathize, he laid down the ancient diadem with an air of painful embarrassment. Scott, whispered, 'Pray forgive me;' and turning round at that moment, observed his daughter deadly pale, and leaning by the door. He immediately drew her out of the room, and when the air had somewhat recovered her, walked with her across the Mound to Castle Street. 'He never spoke all the way home,' she said, 'but every now and then I felt his arm tremble; and from that time I fancied he began to treat me more like a woman than a child. I thought he liked me better, too, than he had ever done before.'

EDINBURGH CASTLE FROM PRINCES STREET

PLATE 47

The Mound was just to the left of this view and the Scotts' steps to it from the Castle entrance would have taken them down the street opposite. The house with the two tall chimney-stacks immediately below the Castle Esplanade was originally built by Allan Ramsay for his retirement and later altered by his son.

JOURNAL OF SIR WALTER SCOTT

SIR WALTER SCOTT

February 12 [1829]—W. Lockhart came to breakfast, full of plans for his house, which will make a pretty and romantic habitation. After breakfast the Court claimed its vassal.

As I came out Mr Chambers introduced a pretty little romantic girl to me who possessed a laudable zeal to know a live poet. I went with my fair admirer as far as the new rooms on the Mound, where I looked into the Royal Society's Rooms, then into the Exhibition, in mere unwillingness to work and desire to dawdle away time. Learned that Lord Haddington had bought the Sir Joshua. I wrought hard to-day and made out five pages.

February 13—This morning Col. Hunter Blair breakfasted here with his wife, a very pretty woman, with a good deal of pleasant conversation. She had been in India, and had looked about her to a purpose. I wrote for several hours in the forenoon, but was nervous and drumlie; also I bothered myself about geography; in short, there was trouble, as miners say when the vein of metal is interrupted. Went out at two, and walked, thank God, better than in the winter, which gives me hopes that the failure of the unfortunate limb is only temporary, owing to severe weather. We dined at John Murray's with the Mansfield family. Lady Caroline Murray possesses, I think, the most pleasing taste for music, and is the best singer I ever heard. No temptation to display a very brilliant voice ever leads her aside from truth and simplicity, and besides, she looks beautiful when she sings.

February 14—Wrote in the morning, which begins to be a regular act of duty. It was late ere I got home, and I did not do much. The letters I received were numerous and craved answers, yet the third volume is getting on hooly and fairly. I am twenty leaves before the printers; but Ballantyne's wife is ill, and it is his nature to indulge apprehensions of the worst, which incapacitates him for labour. I cannot help regarding this amiable weakness of the mind with something too nearly allied to contempt. I keep the press behind me at a good distance, and I, like the

> Postboy's horse, am glad to miss
> The lumber of the wheels.

February 16—Stayed at home and laboured all the forenoon. Young Invernahyle called to bid me interest myself about getting a lad of the house of Scott a commission—how is this possible? The last I tried for there was about 3000 on the list—and they say the boy is too old, being twenty-four. I scribbled three or four pages, forbore smoking and whisky and water, and went to the Royal Society. There Sir William Hamilton read an essay, the result of some anatomical investigations, which contained a masked battery against the phrenologists.

February 17—In the morning I sent off copy and proof. I received the melancholy news that James Ballantyne has lost his wife. With his domestic habits the blow is irretrievable. What can he do, poor fellow, at the head of such a family of children! I should not be surprised if he were to give way to despair.

ROYAL INSTITUTION

PLATE 48

Originally built in 1826 to house the museum of the Society of Antiquities, the Society for the Encouragement of Fine Arts in Scotland, and the Royal Society, of which Scott became President in 1820. The Mound (see page 103) came down immediately behind this building, which is now the Royal Scottish Academy.

MEMORIALS OF HIS TIME

Lord Cockburn

IT WAS the rise of the new town that obliterated our old peculiarities with the greatest rapidity and effect. It not only changed our scenes and habits of life, but, by the mere inundation of modern population, broke up and, as was then thought, vulgarized our prescriptive gentilities.

For example, Saint Cecilia's Hall was the only public resort of the musical, and besides being our most selectly fashionable place of amusement, was the best and the most beautiful concert room I have ever yet seen. And there have I myself seen most of our literary and fashionable gentlemen, predominating with their side curls, and frills, and ruffles, and silver buckles; and our stately matrons stiffened in hoops, and gorgeous satin; and our beauties with high-heeled shoes, powdered and pomatumed hair, and lofty and composite head dresses. All this was in the Cowgate! the last retreat now-a-days of destitution and disease. The building still stands, though raised and changed, and is looked down upon from South Bridge, over the eastern side of the Cowgate Arch. When I last saw it, it seemed to be partly an old-clothesman's shop, and partly a brazier's. The abolition of this Cecilian temple, and the necessity of finding accommodation where they could, and of depending for patronage on the common boisterous public, of course extinguished the delicacies of the old artificial parterre.

Our balls, and their manners, fared no better. The ancient dancing establishments in the Bow, and the Assembly Close, I know nothing about. Every thing of the kind was meant to be annihilated by the erection (about 1784) of the handsome apartments in George Street. Yet even against these, the new part of the old town made a gallant struggle, and in my youth the whole fashionable dancing, as indeed the fashionable every-thing, clung to George Square; where (in Buccleuch Place, close by the south-eastern corner of the square) most beautiful rooms were erected, which, for several years, threw the New Town piece of presumption entirely into the shade. And here were the last remains of the ball-room discipline of the preceding age. Martinet dowagers and venerable beaux acted as masters and mistresses of ceremonies, and made all the preliminary arrangements. No couple could dance unless each party was provided with a ticket prescribing the precise place, in the precise dance. If there was no ticket, the gentleman, or the lady, was dealt with as an intruder, and turned out of the dance. If the ticket had marked upon it—say for a country dance, the figures 3. 5; this meant that the holder was to place himself in the 3d dance, and 5th from the top; and if he was anywhere else, he was set right, or excluded. And the partner's ticket must correspond. Woe on the poor girl who with ticket 2. 7, was found opposite a youth marked 5. 9! It was flirting without a license, and looked very ill, and would probably be reported by the ticket director of that dance to the mother. Of course parties, or parents, who wished to secure dancing for themselves or those they had charge of, provided themselves with correct and corresponding vouchers before the ball day arrived. This could only be accomplished through a director; and the election of a pope sometimes required less jobbing. When parties chose to take their chance, they might do so, but still, though only obtained in the room, the written permission was necessary; and such a thing as a compact to dance, by a couple without official authority, would have been an outrage that could scarcely be contemplated.

ASSEMBLY ROOMS, GEORGE STREET

PLATE 49

*The portico and arcade were added in 1818, shortly before
Cockburn began his reminiscences. The interior of St Cecilia's
Hall, designed in 1763, has now been restored—the building
belongs to the University of Edinburgh.*

LECTURES ON ARCHITECTURE AND PAINTING

JOHN RUSKIN

I THINK myself peculiarly happy in being permitted to address the citizens of Edinburgh on the subject of architecture, for it is one which, they cannot but feel, interests them nearly. Of all the cities in the British Islands, Edinburgh is the one which presents most advantages for the display of a noble building; and which, on the other hand, sustains most injury in the erection of a commonplace or unworthy one. You are all proud of your city; surely you must feel it a duty in some sort to justify your pride; that is to say, to give yourselves a *right* to be proud of it. That you were born under the shadow of its two fantastic mountains,—that you live where from your room windows you can trace the shores of its glittering Firth, are no rightful subjects of pride. You did not raise the mountains, nor shape the shores; and the historical houses of your Canongate, and the broad battlements of your castle, reflect honour upon you only through your ancestors. Before you boast of your city, before even you venture to call it *yours*, ought you not scrupulously to weigh the exact share you have had in adding to it or adorning it, to calculate seriously the influence upon its aspect which the work of your own hands has exercised? I do not say that, even when you regard your city in this scrupulous and testing spirit, you have not considerable grounds for exultation. As far as I am acquainted with modern architecture, I am aware of no streets which, in simplicity and manliness of style, or general breadth and brightness of effect, equal those of the New Town of Edinburgh. But your feelings of pleasure and pride in them are much complicated with those which are excited entirely by the surrounding scenery. As you walk up or down George Street, for instance, do you not look eagerly for every opening to the north and south, which lets in the lustre of the Firth of Forth, or the rugged outline of the Castle Rock? Take away the sea waves, and the dark basalt, and I fear you would find little to interest you in George Street by itself.

GEORGE STREET LOOKING EAST

PLATE 50

The turning off to the right is Frederick Street, with the facade of the Assembly Rooms beyond (see also plate 49). Hanover Street goes off to the left (or north), and beyond it is St Andrew's Church (see also plate 34). At the end of the street is St Andrew Square and the Melville Monument. The house in which Shelley lodged (see page 76) was No. 60, which is midway between Frederick Street and the Assembly Rooms, on the right. To find it, Hogg would therefore have come up Hanover Street from Princes Street.

MEMOIRS OF A HIGHLAND LADY

ELIZABETH GRANT OF ROTHIEMURCHUS

IN MAY we removed to Charlotte Square, a house I found the most agreeable of any we had ever lived in in Edinburgh; the shrubbery in front, and the peep from the upper windows at the back, of the Firth of Forth with its wooded shores and distant hills, made the look-out so cheerful. We were in the midst, too, of our friends. We made two new acquaintance, the Wolfe Murrays next door, and Sir James and Lady Henrietta Ferguson in my father's old house, in which Jane and I were born. Nothing could be pleasanter than our sociable life. The gaiety was over, but every day some meeting took place between us young people. My mother's tea-table was, I think, the general gathering point. In the mornings we made walking parties, and one day we went to Rosslyn and Lasswade, a merry company. Another day we spent at sea.

The Captain of the frigate lying in the roads gallantly determined to make a return to Edinburgh for all the attention Edinburgh had paid him. He invited all left of his winter acquaintance to a breakfast and dance on board. We drove down to the pier at Newhaven in large merry parties, where now the splendid Granton pier shames its predecessors, and there found boats awaiting us, such a gay little fleet, manned by sailors in their best suits, and we were rowed quickly across the sparkling water, for it was a beautiful day, and hoisted up upon the deck. There was an awning spread, flags, etc., waving, a quadrille and a military band all ready, and Jane, who was in high good looks, soon took her place among the dancers, having been engaged by the little monkey of a middy who had piloted us over. The collation was below, all along the lower deck; we sat down to it at four o'clock, and then danced on again till midnight, plentifully served with refreshments hospitably pressed upon us by our entertainers. Sailors are so hearty, and every officer of the ship seemed to feel he had the part of host to play. There never was a merrier *fête*. . . .

We were, like the best bred of the company, in half dress, with frocks made half high and with long sleeves. Jane's frock was abundantly flounced, but it had no other trimming; she wore a white belt, and had a hanging bunch of lilacs with a number of green leaves in her hair. My frock was white, too, but all its flounces were headed with pink ribbon run through muslin, a pink sash, and all my load of hair quite plain. A few unhappy girls were in full dress, short sleeves, low necks, white satin shoes. Miss Cochrane, the Admiral's daughter, was the most properly dressed amongst us; she was more accustomed to the sort of thing. She wore a white well-frilled petticoat, an open silk spencer, and a little Swiss hat, from one side of which hung a bunch of roses. She and the dress together conquered Captain Dalling; they were married a few months after.

CHARLOTTE SQUARE, WEST SIDE 1819

PLATE 51

The Grant family occupied the house she describes here for only a few weeks in 1817. At that time the Post Office Directory records an advocate called Wolfe Murray living in No. 17, which was then, as it still is, the house next to St George's Church (now West Register Office) in this view. The Grant's house was therefore No. 16, the one on the right of the view, two doors up from Lord Cockburn, who lived in No. 14. Elizabeth Grant was born in No. 6 Charlotte Square, now the official residence of the Secretary of State for Scotland.

NOCTES AMBROSIANAE

CHRISTOPHER NORTH (Professor John Wilson)

TICKLER I think I shall put on my clothes again, James. The air is chill; and I see from your face that the water is cold as ice.

SHEPHERD Oh, man! but you're a desperate cooart. Think shame o' yoursel, stannin naked there, at the mouth 'o the machine, wi' the haill crew o' yon brig sailin up the Firth looking at ye, ane after anither, frae cyuck to captain, through the telescope.

TICKLER James, on the sincerity of a shepherd, and the faith of a Christian, lay your hand on your heart, and tell me, was not the shock tremendous? I thought you never would have reappeared.

SHEPHERD The shock was naething, nae mair than what a body feels when waukening suddenly during a sermon, or fa'in ower a staircase in a dream.—But I'm aff to Inchkeith.

TICKLER Whizz. [*Flings a somerset into the sea.*

SHEPHERD Ane—twa—three—four—five—sax—seven— aught—but there's nae need o' coontin—for nae pearl-diver, in the Straits o' Madagascar or aff the coast o' Coromandel, can haud his breath like Tickler. Weel, that's surprisin. Yon chaise has gane about half a mile o' gate towards Portybelly sin' he gaed fizzin outower the lugs like a verra rocket. Safe us! what's this gruppin me by the legs? A sherk—a sherk—a sherk!

TICKLER (*yellowing to the surface*) Blabla—blabla—bla—

SHEPHERD He's kept soomin aneath the water till he's sick; but every man for himsel, and God for us a'—I'm aff.

[SHEPHERD *stretches away to sea in the direction of Inchkeith*—TICKLER *in pursuit.*

TICKLER Every sinew, my dear James, like so much whipcord. I swim like a salmon.

SHEPHERD Oh, sir! that Lord Byron had but been alive the noo, what a sweepstakes!

TICKLER A Liverpool gentleman has undertaken, James, to swim four-and-twenty miles at a stretch. What are the odds?

SHEPHERD Three to one on Saturn and Neptune. He'll get numm.

TICKLER James, I had no idea you were so rough on the back. You're a perfect otter.

SHEPHERD Nae personality, Mr Tickler, out at sea. I'll compare carcasses wi' you ony day o' the year. Yet, you're a gran' soomer—out o' the water at every stroke, neck, breast, shouthers, and half-way doun the back—after the fashion o' the great American serpent. As for me, my style o' soomin's less showy—laigh and lown—less hurry, but mair speed. Come. sir, I'll dive you for a jug o' toddy.

[TICKLER *and* SHEPHERD *melt away like foam-bells in the sunshine.*

SHEPHERD Mr Tickler!

TICKLER James!

SHEPHERD It's a drawn bate—sae we'll baith pay.—Oh, sir! Isna Embro' a glorious city? Sae clear the air, yonner you see a man and a woman stannin on the tap o' Arthur's Seat! I had nae notion there were sae many steeples, and spires, and columms, and pillars, and obelisks, and doms, in Embro'! And at this distance the ee canna distinguish atween them that belangs to kirks, and them that belangs to naval monuments, and them that belangs to ile-gas companies, and them that's only chimley-heids in the auld toun, and the taps o' groves, or single trees, sic as poplars; and aboon a' and ahint a', craigs and saft-broo'd hills sprinkled wi' sheep, lichts and shadows, and the blue vapoury glimmer o' a Midsummer day—het, het, het, wi the barometer at ninety; but here, to us twa, bob-bobbin amang the fresh, cool, murmurin, and faemy wee waves, temperate as the air within the mermaid's palace. Anither dive!

EDINBURGH ACROSS THE FIRTH OF FORTH *c.*1825

PLATE 52

This piece about swimming off the Leith coast appeared in
Blackwood's Magazine in July 1827. Inchkeith is a tiny island
in the middle of the Firth just off to the left, or east, of this view.

MY SCHOOLS AND SCHOOLMASTERS

HUGH MILLER

MANY A long-cherished association drew my thoughts to Edinburgh. I was acquainted with Ramsay, and Fergusson, and the *Humphrey Clinker* of Smollett, and had read a description of the place in the *Marmion* and the earlier novels of Scott; and I was not yet too old to feel as if I were approaching a great magical city—like some of those in the *Arabian Nights*—that was even more intensely poetical than Nature itself. I did somewhat chide the tantalizing mist, that, like a capricious showman, now raised one corner of its curtain, and anon another, and showed me the place at once very indistinctly, and only by bits at a time; and yet I know not that I could in reality have seen it to greater advantage, or after a mode more in harmony with my previous conceptions. The water in the harbour was too low, during the first hour or two after our arrival, to float our vessel, and we remained tacking in the roadstead, watching for the signal from the pier-head which was to intimate to us when the tide had risen high enough for our addmission; and so I had sufficient time given to me to con over the features of the scene, as presented in detail. At one time a flat reach of the New Town came full into view, along which, in the general dimness, the multitudinous chimneys stood up like stacks of corn in a field newly reaped; at another, the Castle loomed out dark in the cloud; then, as if suspended over the earth, the rugged summit of Arthur's Seat came strongly out, while its base still remained invisible in the wreath; and anon I caught a glimpse of the distant Pentlands, enveloped by a clear blue sky, and lighted up by the sun.

EDINBURGH FROM LEITH *c.*1825

PLATE 53

Miller came to Edinburgh in 1824.

CADDIE WILLIE

Douglas M'Ewan

ONE OF the strangest peculiarities of this eccentric old caddie was the way in which he wore his clothes. He may be said to have literally carried his wardrobe with him wherever he went. All the clothes he got he put on his back, *one suit above another*. To admit of his wearing three or four coats at once, he had to cut out the sleeves to let them on. True to the uniform which invariably distinguished golfers in those days, an old red coat was always worn outside of them all. He also wore three or four vests, an old worn fur one being outermost. It was the same with his trousers—three or four pairs on, and the worst outermost; and three bonnets, sewed one within the other!

When Willie first came from the Highlands, he had been in the habit of going about the country selling tracts; and happening to come to Edinburgh, and passing through Bruntsfield Links, he stood to look at the golfers. It being a busy golfing day, the golfers could not all get caddies, and one of them asked Willie to carry his clubs; which he did, and got a shilling for his hour's work. With an eye to the main chance, Willie forthwith took to the Royal and Ancient Game; and in order to be near the Links, took up his quarters at Bruntsfield, renting a garret from Mr John Brand, gardener, lessee of the lands and mansion-houses of Leven Lodge and Valleyfield. Willie was very honest, paying his rent regularly, and for his bread and milk as he got it. He lived entirely on baps and milk, never having a warm diet, or a fire in his garret, even in the coldest winter. He was always happy and cheerful. I was a favourite of his, as, when I saw the caddie boys annoying him, I used to say that I would tell the gentlemen of their conduct, which had the effect of stopping them. They knew that the gentlemen would not employ them if it was known that they annoyed Willie.

Possessed of an inborn love of sport, Willie used to go to the village fairs round about Edinburgh with a view to picking up a few pence. His apparatus for enticing th youth of a sporting turn was exceedingly simple consisting of three turned pieces of wood about a foo long, with turned base about one and a half or two inche in diameter, something like what you see in milliners windows to put their caps and bonnets on. Cutting thre holes in the earth the size of the base of his sticks, in th form of a triangle, he put a penny on the top of each stick He had a wand about three feet long. The player stoo about ten feet off; and paying a penny for his shot, tried t skim the pennies off the top, which was very seldon done; the wand either going too high and missing, or to low and knocking away the sticks, when the pennie dropped into the holes—either result being equally i Willie's favour. I will never forget Willie's face and hi happy chuckle as he used to cry out, 'All in the hole! Many people were attracted around Willie by his odc appearance, and tried their skill at his pennies for the sak of giving him a few coppers. These village fairs were great treat to us boys. They were called Carters' Plays and were looked forward to by all the lads and lasses fo miles round about, as the great event of the year; ther being a grand equestrian procession, when both men anc horses were laden with ribbons and flowers. The lasse vied with each other who would turn out thei sweethearts with the grandest display of ribbons anc flowers. It was a great pleasure to visit the villages oi these occasions, and to see so many happy people.

Gunn was in the habit of going to his Highland home every autumn, selling his tracts by the way, and wa generally away about six weeks. The last time he bade m good-bye (which was about the year 1820), he told tha he had as much money saved as would pay his funera expenses, as he had a horror of a pauper's burial. Fron this journey poor Willie never returned. All the inquiry the golfers made, they could never learn his fate.

BRUNTSFIELD LINKS IN THE EARLY 1820s,
WITH THE CASTLE BEHIND

PLATE 54

*Is the curiously garbed figure in the middle foreground Caddie
Willie himself? His attitude, the description and the dates all fit.*

ON LAYING THE FOUNDATION STONE OF ST BERNARD'S WELL

CLAUDERO (James Wilson)

NO MUSE I invoke to help out my song,
The muses all flutter around in a throng;
A theme so delightful with transport they view,
And with their assistance my song I pursue.
Great Drummond improveth what nature doth send,
To country and city he's always a friend?
Regardless of junto's his lordship pursues
The weal of the public in all that he does;
Unwearied he studies the good of the town,
And success his labours for ever must crown,
Though opposed of late by Bedlamite Tom,
Who ne'er could do good abroad nor at home;
And likewise by others of far better fame;
What views they had in it my muse shall not name.
    With pity he saw the diseas'd without aid,
(Physicians do nothing unless they are paid)
Then straight thro' three kingdoms he sent for supply,
And rear'd up the structure, called Infirmary,
Where ev'ry disease that physicians can cure
Is instantly heal'd, for the rich or the poor.
When heav'n, propitious to grant his desire
To th' utmost extent his heart could require,
For the health of the poor sent this sanative well
A blessing to all that around it do dwell.

That as the foundations of one he did lay;
The other should likewise be put in his way,
His pious endeavours to crown in his day.
    Persevere still, Great Sir! and be not dismay'd,
Nor regard the harangues that against you are made.
Mad Tom loud may rave; he may curse, he may swear
When with sinful Marg'ret he's quaffing his beer,
Cry out 'gainst your scheme for bringing in water,
And get posses of ale-wives to join in his clatter:
But the good of the city being your chief intent,
And on schemes for the public your mind being bent,
Despise the poor crew, go on with full speed,
And prosperity surely will bless you when dead.
    This water so healthful near Ed'nburgh doth rise,
Which not only Bath, but Moffat outvies,
Most diseases of nature it quickly doth cure,
Except the disease that is got from a whore.
It cleans the intestines, and appetite gives,
While morbific matter it quite away drives:
Its amazing effects cannot be deny'd,
And drugs are quite useless where it is apply'd:
So what doctors can't cure is done by this Spring,
Reserv'd till this year of great Drummond's reign.

ST BERNARD'S WELL

PLATE 55

*The poem is dated 1760, the year in which the spring was
discovered. The structure was erected in 1789 by the eccentric
lawyer Lord Gardenstone, who used to sleep with a pig. The
statue inside it was replaced in 1888.*

FAREWEEL, EDINBURGH

BARONESS NAIRNE

FAREWEEL, Edinburgh, where happy we hae been,
Fareweel, Edinburgh, Caledonia's Queen!
Auld Reekie, fare-ye-weel, and Reekie New beside,
Ye're like a chieftain grim and gray, wi' a young bonny bride.
Fareweel, Edinburgh, and your trusty volunteers,
Your Council, a' sae circumspect, your Provost without peers,
The auld toun-guard, sae neat and trim, sae honest and sae sour,
Aye stannin' near the auld St Giles, that plays and tells the hour.

Fareweel, Edinburgh, your philosophic men;
Your scribes that set you a' to richts, and wield the golden pen;
The Session-court, your thrang resort, big wigs and lang gowns a';
An' if ye dinna keep the peace, it's no for want o' law.
Fareweel, Edinburgh, and a' your glittering wealth;
Your Bernard's Well, your Calton Hill, where every breeze is health;
An' spite o' a' your fresh sea-gales, should ony chance to dee,
It's no for want o' recipe, the doctor, or the fee.

WATER OF LEITH AND ST BERNARD'S WELL *c.*1825

PLATE 56

*Beyond the Well is St Bernard's Church, built in 1823 in what
is now Saxe-Coburg Street. Above and to the right are the New
Town houses of Moray Place.*

Fareweel, Edinburgh, your hospitals and ha's,
The rich man's friend, the Cross lang ken'd, auld Ports, and City wa's;
The kirks that grace their honoured place, now peacefu' as they stand,
Where'er they're found, on Scottish ground, the bulwarks of the land.
Fareweel, Edinburgh, your sons o' genius fine,
That send your name on wings o' fame beyond the burnin' line;
A name that's stood maist since the flood, and just when it's forgot
Your bard will be forgotten too, your ain Sir Walter Scott.

Fareweel, Edinburgh, and a' your daughters fair;
Your Palace in the sheltered glen, your Castle in the air;
Your rocky brows, your grassy knowes, and eke your mountain bauld;
Were I to tell your beauties a', my tale would ne'er be tauld;
Fareweel, Edinburgh, whar happy we hae been;
Fareweel, Edinburgh, Caledonia's Queen!
Prosperity to Edinburgh, wi' every rising sun,
An' blessin's be on Edinburgh till time his race has run!

EDINBURGH FROM THE EAST *c.*1825

PLATE 57

*The buildings on the sky-line are, from left to right: Royal
Infirmary, Heriot's Hospital, Tron Church, St Giles', the
'Castle in the air', St Cuthbert's Church, New Jail, Nelson's
Monument. The 'Palace in the sheltered glen' is just beyond the
trees.*

SOURCES OF ILLUSTRATIONS

The illustrations in *A Book of Old Edinburgh*
are taken from the following works:

VIEWS IN EDINBURGH AND ITS VICINITY: drawn and engraved by J and H S Storer
(published by A Constable and Co., Edinburgh, 2 vols, 1820)

Plate numbers 3, 4, 10, 11, 13, 14, 16, 18, 19, 20, 23, 26, 28,
30, 32, 33, 34, 35, 37, 43, 49, 51, 55; pages 1, 2, 86, 102

PICTURESQUE VIEWS OF EDINBURGH: the drawings by J Ewbank, engraved by W H Lizars
(printed for Daniel Lizars, Edinburgh 1825)

Plate numbers 1, 2, 12, 15, 24, 25, 29, 31, 38, 39, 41,
44, 45, 46, 47, 50, 52, 53, 54, 56, 57; pages 6, 9

MEMORIALS OF EDINBURGH IN THE OLDEN TIME by Daniel Wilson FRSSA
(published by Hugh Paton, Adam Square, Edinburgh, 2 vols, 1848)

Drawn by Daniel Wilson, engraved as indicated: plate numbers 5 (W Forrest), 6 (W Forrest),
7 (T Steuart), 8 (T Steuart), 9 (T Steuart), 17 (W. Forrest), 22 (T Steuart): pages 3, 58 (from J Gordon);
127, 128 (drawn by H Dudley); map (adapted by J Murray)

SCOTLAND by William Beattie MD
(published by George Virtue, 26 Ivy Lane, Paternoster Row, London 1848)

Drawn and engraved as indicated: plate numbers 27 (T Allom, W Woolnoth),
36 (T Allom, H Adlard), 40 (W H Bartlett, H Griffiths), 48 (G M Kemp, W Deeble)

INDEX OF PLACES

mentioned in the captions to illustrations

*Capital of the
old Mercat Cross*

INDEX OF AUTHORS

The house in High Street, opposite Tron Church, where until 1725 Allan Ramsay carried on his business as author, publisher and bookseller.